FROM POISONED STEW TO PASTURES NEW

*The Story of Pastor Emmanuel Nnyanzi of Mbarara
and Parental Care Ministries Uganda*

Mary Weeks Millard

Published by Zaccmedia
www.zaccmedia.com
info@zaccmedia.com

Published April 2016

ISBN: 978-1-911211-30-3

British Library Cataloguing-in-Publication Data
A catalogue record for this book is available from the British Library.

Zaccmedia aims to produce books that will help to extend and build up the Kingdom
of God. We do not necessarily agree with every view expressed by the authors, or
with every interpretation of Scripture expressed. We expect readers to make their
own judgment in the light of their understanding of God's Word and in an attitude of
Christian love and fellowship.

CONTENTS

DEDICATION

This book is dedicated to all the 'Precious Promises' within the Parental Care Ministries (PCM) family. May each one of you continue to live within the circle of God's love and share this love with the people you meet as you journey through life.

~

To be designated as an 'orphan' in Uganda brings a stigma which opens the door to abuse of all kinds. The children within the PCM family are never known as orphans, but as precious promises – for that is indeed what they are – each life is a precious promise from God.

ACKNOWLEDGMENTS

My grateful thanks to Pastor Emmy and Sarah Nnyanzi, who have been such an inspiration to me and many others. It is such a privilege to share their story.

I also want to thank all who have been willing to share their stories:

Nigel and Marian Whitaker of PCM UK; Precious Promises Esther and Julius; Julian Nsabamukama; Peter Frith; Tracey Lloyd; Fraim; Pastor Charles and Grace Ochwo; Grace (Nnyanzi) Nowamani; Chris and Sophie Spree; Beatrice Kabaali.

My thanks, too, go to Patrick Butler and Dr. Mark and Monica Barret for allowing me to use information from the book, *So Much More*, written about PCM USA.

Many thanks to Hugh Henderson, MBE, Director of Mission International, for being willing to write the foreword for this book.

Also my grateful thanks to my beloved husband, Rev. Malcolm Millard, for all his advice and patience throughout this project.

FOREWORD

This story for me starts back in October 1989 when I first visited Uganda. I was a young agricultural lecturer who had been asked to visit Uganda to see if there was any way that I could help in an agricultural project. I had two weeks holiday from college and so, along with the late Stuart Brunton, I headed off to a country and a continent I had never visited before. The seed for this visit had been planted when I was a child. Missionaries on furlough would visit our small church, and with the use of slides, they would regale stories of missions in Africa. I suppose that was when the positive response to the request for me to go there was initiated.

A challenging trip was to become yet more challenging when I was told, upon reaching Lugazi, that there was no agriculture project, but there was to be "a series of twenty-four seminars to be taught to church leaders, starting tomorrow!" Well, it was then that my agricultural career was to take a major detour.

One of the delegates at this and successive leaders' training events, at which I and others were called upon to teach, was Pastor Emmy Nnyanzi from Mbarara in southwestern Uganda. Initially he was quite unknown to me, merging into the crowd of black faces and bodies in oversized suits. He first became known when he boldly asked if I would come to Mbarara and preach there. The idea of a trip to the deep, dark south was something not to be missed by some, but for me, it was something I didn't really relish that much. Eventually I agreed to go, so I found myself in Mbarara the following year, preaching in a tiny church made of sticks, tarpaulins and polythene sheeting. These 'small beginnings' were challenging, yet inspiring. The Mzungu (white man) was a hit with these dear people and they responded well to the fledgling young preacher!

Year after year went past and after many visits there were obvious changes and developments to the growing ministry which was to become Parental Care Ministries, headed by Pastor Emmy. The church ministry had child care and education in its DNA. The challenges to find support to educate children, in particular girls who were predominately kept at home to carry water for parents with AIDS and other sicknesses or to look after recently bereaved grandparents who were unable to carry water from the water source, which could be many miles away. Pastor Emmy would try to find ways and alternatives to encourage families to release their children to attend school. The struggle was huge and long; yet there was a measure of success. Soon the school began to grow, as the little kids from the primary school graduated to become the big kids in the secondary school.

The whole ministry ran on a shoestring, a broken shoestring at times, because there were times when the funds ran out and major decisions had to be made so that the ministry could remain alive and the vision to provide a vibrant church and a healthy school could continue. These were days of learning to hold on to God's purpose and to hold firm to the vision He had given. I will be honest. I don't know how he and his lovely wife, Sarah, made it, particularly in the early days. By this time I was involved in full-time mission work and there was a limit to the support which could be provided – but make it they did!

After some years, a short visit to the UK was to be the next turning point in this growing and developing ministry. Friends in England, Wales and Scotland joined together to provide a tour for Emmy and

Sarah, These friendships were to introduce the next phase of the work. Sadly, it was a time in which I could no longer be so deeply involved as I had been previously, due to the way that my service for the Lord had been routed. However, I watch with interest as Parental Care Ministries continues to grow and develop, now with partners in the USA, too.

This is a remarkable story – a story of God at work in the lives of a genuinely authentic and committed family. This story, if nothing else, will cast a challenge to those who read it, a challenge that relying on God in all circumstances, with no one or nothing else to fall back on is the best policy and the only way to achieve lasting, eternal and godly success.

Hugh Henderson MBE
CEO Mission International

Dundee, June 2015

INTRODUCTION

My first taste of life in Africa came in 1965, when, as a newly qualified nurse and midwife, I took an appointment with the Medical Research Council of U.K. in Kampala, Uganda. I was based at what was then Old Mulago Hospital, the old buildings which had preceded the new Mulago Hospital, a gift to Uganda from the British government to mark her independence, having been a Protectorate of Great Britain.

I was working at the Infant Malnutrition Research Centre. We were a one-ward-and-laboratory unit with a small, close-knit staff.

From the moment I stepped off the VC10 airplane I felt a thrill and a sense of excitement and knew I would love living in, as Sir Winston Churchill called Uganda, 'the Pearl of Africa.' At that time I had no inkling of the big part that Africa would play in my life. By the time my contract had ended I was engaged to marry a missionary, Philip Weeks, who was working in the West Nile district. After our marriage, we returned to work in what was then Zaire, now the Democratic Republic of Congo, with the Africa Inland Mission, now AIM International. In 1970 we returned to UK and my husband continued to work in mission with Scripture Union until the condition, Multi-systems Atrophy, from which he suffered, had made him too disabled to continue working.

After his death in 2000, I sensed the Lord was saying to me that he was leading me into a new season of my life. Soon after that my home church hosted a meeting for the small mission, Signpost International. From that meeting an opportunity arose for me to travel to Rwanda with Signpost in November 2001. That initial visit has led to fourteen years of short -term mission and involvement in the Great Lakes area of Africa. It has been a huge privilege for me.

The team leader for Signpost was Hugh Henderson – a great man of God who is now the CEO of Mission International UK, and who kindly agreed to write the foreword for this book.

Hugh had travelled several times to Uganda and on one of these visits had met and made friends with Pastor Emmanuel (Emmy) Nnyanzi and his wife, Sarah. Such was their friendship that when Hugh was leading a team in Rwanda, Emmy and Sarah made the journey from Mbarara to Kigali to visit him. It was there that I was introduced to an amazing young couple. Emmy and Sarah have a gift for making friends and our friendship has continued to this day.

Hugh had told me that Emmy's ear was close to God and he often had dreams and words of revelation which were from the Lord, so when, a few months later, Emmy emailed and told me that he had dreamt that I was with him in the villages around Mbarara, preaching and teaching, I had to take it seriously. After praying, I arranged to visit the Nnyanzi family in Mbarara for a week.

That week's visit was perhaps a turning point in all our lives. Being a widow and by then in my early sixties, it was a great journey of faith to venture alone to Uganda. My family were also hesitant about letting their mother travel so far on her own. I was going 'up country' and the roads of Uganda have quite a reputation for accidents! I had not been to Uganda since 1970, over thirty years previous to this trip.

I arrived safely at Entebbe Airport and the heat almost overwhelmed me – I had forgotten how much hotter it was in

Uganda than in Rwanda! I went into the arrivals hall to be met by a beaming Emmy and all my fears evaporated.

That visit was a challenge for Pastor Emmy, too. Where was this elderly Mzungu (white person) going to sleep? She could hardly sleep in their one-bedroom, mud-brick house which already housed two adults and eight children! Emmy was unhappy about putting me into a hotel on my own. That could also be a very unsafe place for me, as a white person can be a target for thieves. In faith Emmy rented a small brick-built house for a month. It was very basic, just a few rooms with shared washing-toilet facilities, but the Nnyanzi children were very excited. For them it was like living in a palace and they wanted to stay there for good!

It was an exciting visit, and for me a very new experience to go out into the villages on preaching crusades. Even in my years as a missionary, my role had been working in a hospital, not itinerant evangelism. I was thrilled to see God at work and thrilled to visit small churches, which Emmy and Sarah had planted, and also a school at Ishongororo, which continues to this day. Towards the end of that time I begged Emmy and Sarah to take me to see their own home. When I saw the tiny mud-brick house with the tin roof I could hardly take it in. It was so small and so poor and not even their own. Emmy confessed that sometimes the landlord tried to drive them away because they were overdue with their rent.

As Bagandan missionaries to the Ankole people they lived by faith and had no regular salary. I heard stories of the days when they had almost nothing with which to feed the children and they all went to bed after just a drink of tea. They lived from hand to mouth, trusting God to look after them. It touched my heart so much to hear about their 'normal' lives and I began to pray for something better for them.

During that week we all began to dream. I felt the Lord say to me that He would make Emmy the 'head and not the tail. I talked with Sarah. She dreamed of having a farm one day. We looked at cattle as we walked in the countryside. How far from her present reality that dream seemed!

We talked about the church in Mbarara, which was housed in a broken-down building with noisy storks residing on the tin roof and the rent being so high! We even dared to visit an estate agent and look at the prices of houses, not having any idea how God might give them a house of their own!

As a treat, at the end of my stay, I was able to take the family to the Queen Elizabeth Game Park. We left Mbarara in an old, hired minibus and set off in great excitement. It was wonderful for the children to see the animals which, even only thirty years before, had roamed free in the countryside.

It proved to be a long, hot day, and we all arrived home very tired. It was one of those days that make memories for children, and we were all very happy. However, that night I became sick. Maybe it was dehydration, but during the night I was throwing up. I tried to cross the yard to the communal toilet, and found Emmy was outside my room. I had no idea, but he had kept watch over me the whole trip in case anyone tried to come at night and steal my belongings. I will never forget his love and care as he helped me that night, and the Lord used the story of his care to touch people in UK, too.

On my return to my home, I was thrilled at what God had done during that trip but also burdened for the Nnyanzi family and particularly their living conditions as they returned to the mud brick house.

Almost as soon as I had settled back, I needed to visit the building and replacement window firm who had done a lot of work on my house. The original owner of the firm had died a few months after the death of my husband, and his wife had taken over the management. Her four children were also working in the family firm. I went to the office to talk about the replacement window I needed and was greeted by the widow and her eldest daughter, both of whom attended the same church that I did. They asked me about the trip and I told them about all the wonderful things which happened, but also about the Nnyanzi family home and even the visit to the estate agent. They were very moved and suggested that we try to raise money to buy a house, promptly promising £1,000 to start the fund!

I went on my way praising the Lord! My faith was encouraged by their generosity. My next stop that morning was for a check-up with my doctor. Again, my G.P. asked about my health on the trip and I told her about the visit to the Game Park and the night which followed. This led to me explaining about the house in which we were staying and why we were there, as well as my concerns for Emmy, Sarah and the children. She looked at me for a moment and then got out her cheque book.

"This month I received a bonus in my pay packet. I would like to give that to you to help this family," she said. I gasped when I looked at the cheque – it was for another £1000! By this time I knew that the Lord was going to do a miracle and provide a house for this dear family!

I had been trying to sell my house for a while. I put it on the market soon after my husband's death, because not only was it too large for my needs and had been especially adapted for wheelchair use, which someone else might badly need, but I also had very little money and needed to release some capital. It had seemed that no one wanted to buy my house, but within days of arriving home, not only did I have a buyer, but also saw a very suitable property where I could live. The result was that within a few weeks I was able to add the tithe from my sale to the now rapidly growing fund for the house. Within three months of my visit to Mbarara, there was around £15,000 to send to Emmy, and the family were able to buy a house. Not only did this give the family a secure base, it also released Emmy and Sarah to be able to open their home to needy orphaned or abandoned children, to give them parental love and care.

The following year I was able to visit them in their new home. It was such a joy! Their own children were looking stronger and better, and what is more, the garage was full of children! I thought perhaps they had enough young ones around them to clothe, feed and educate, and remember telling Emmy so – but his faith and vision were far greater than mine--and this was the start of Parental Care Ministries. Emmy and Sarah just wanted to give to any children who needed it, the love and care which they did not receive themselves as children.

By this time Sarah had already started a small school in a mud church on the outskirts of Mbarara. It was called the Henderson School, as an honour to Hugh Henderson and the encouragement he had given to Emmy.

Having their own house also led to another development. They were now in a position to host teams of young people and a team went from UK, sent by Signpost International and led by Hugh. Then a young sixteen-year-old girl, Laura Whitaker, went on a visit arranged by St. David's College, Llandudno, Wales, for a week to Mbarara. From this visit sprang in God's good time, Parental Care Ministries UK. Laura's story and that of her parents will be shared later in this book as well as my growing involvement.

It has been a privilege for me to see this ministry grow over the years – to have been a link in the chain helping so many needy children in Uganda. I hope this book will inspire others to also become links and forge an even stronger chain, to God's glory!

Chapter One

THE STORY OF ESTHER AND JULIUS, TWO PRECIOUS PROMISES

Matthew19:13-14 (NIV)

"Then little children were brought to Jesus for him to place his hands on them and pray for them. But the disciples rebuked those who brought them. Jesus said, 'Let the little children come to me, and do not hinder them, for the kingdom of heaven belongs to such as these.' When he had placed his hands on them, he went on from there."

At a time and in a society when children had no rights and were often considered just the property of their parents, Jesus made it very clear that they were important to Him and to His Father, God. Sadly, over 2000 years later, many children all over the world are still treated as things, rather than as people, and their rights are being ignored. Stories of child abduction and slavery are common today, as are stories of neglect and abuse.

Those who have suffered from a lack of parental love and care, for whatever reason, grow up with a great loss inside of them and are often never able to become the people that God intended them to be when He planned and created them. Psalm 139:13-16 (NIV) reminds us that no child is an 'accident' in His sight. "For you created my inmost being; you knit me together in my mother's womb. I praise you because I am fearfully and wonderfully made; your works are wonderful, I know that full well. My frame was not hidden from you when I was made in the secret place. When I was woven together in the depths of the earth, your eyes saw my unformed body. All the days ordained for me were written in your book before one of them came to be."

Sometimes the neglect and abandonment grows out of the pain and circumstances of the parents, and this was partly the case for a little girl and her half-brother in Uganda. In 2002 this little girl was born in Uganda. She was given the name of Esitheri – Esther. We cannot know what her mother was feeling or how her life was at that time. Many young women have no choice regarding who will be their husband. Marriages are often arranged between families without any consideration given to the happiness of the girl, but as just a financial arrangement for the family. Esther's mother ran away and left her child with her husband when she was only one year old. Esther's father was polygamous and was already married to another woman who bore him a son, Julius, just one year younger than Esther.

Esther's father, left with a one-year-old child, took her to his mother and asked her to take care of the baby, which she did for three-and-a-half years. When she was four-and-a-half, Esther's grandmother died and the little girl was then returned to her father's house, but by that time both her father and her stepmother were very sick with HIV/AIDS. It was only a short time after her return to her Dad's home that Esther suffered another loss, for her step-mother died. So Julius was also now bereft of his mother. These two small children were left in the care of a very sick father. Indeed, he was also likely to die. This whole story could have had a very sad ending had it not been for the fact that Julius and Esther's father had a sister called Florence. Florence lived in Mbarara and attended the church whose minister was Pastor Emmy Nnyanzi. Florence was concerned about her brother and his children and came to Emmy and Sarah and begged them to help. They agreed to try and help and asked

Florence to go to the village, which was a three-hour journey from Mbarara, and bring her brother and the children to them.

So Esther, Julius and their father were brought by bus to Mbarara. Their father was indeed a very sick man. He begged Emmy and Sarah to take his children into their family and school, for he feared that he didn't have long to live. What must those young children have felt? All they had ever known was abandonment, sickness and death, and now they were taken far from home and the village they knew, to a strange family and a strange town! Their father left the two children and never returned, never phoned to ask after them, never sent a message, never enquired as to their wellbeing. It is now seven years and in spite of being so sick when he left them, he did not die – but just abandoned them!

However, they were received with love and brought into the family of Parental Care Ministries, and have indeed received the love and parental care which is the birthright of every child. Esther has flourished, despite the fact that she has not seen her mother since she was one-year-old or her father for seven years. Even should Julius and Esther now have a surprise visit from their father, they wouldn't be able to recognise him; after so many years he would be a stranger to them. Yet there is no bitterness or resentment in the hearts of these two children. Having been nurtured and educated in an atmosphere of love and taught the gospel of Jesus, they have received Him into their lives and these two young people have been transformed.

They are very happy children. Esther is now thirteen and Julius is twelve. Their hearts are full of love for Jesus and Esther shows great leadership potential. She serves as a worship leader in the children's choir. In April and May 2015 she went to the USA with the Parental Care Ministry children's choir and her testimony was such that many, many hearts were moved as the Holy Spirit spoke through her.

At school Esther has also been a good student. She took her national primary leaving examination in November 2015 and progressed to high school for the new school year in January 2016.

This is just one story that shows how PCM have brought the love of Jesus into the lives of two small children from an insignificant village in Uganda, and how His love has transformed their situation. What is it that has motivated Emmy and Sarah to care so much for children who are orphaned, neglected, abandoned or in very poor circumstances? It had been the transformation of their own lives by that same wonderful love of Jesus.

Specialist social workers that care for children who for one reason or another have experienced a traumatic childhood, will emphasise the need not only for love, but also permanence in their relationships, for children to grow up into an emotionally healthy adulthood. Children who have not experienced the blessing of lasting relationships will be scared to allow themselves to become attached to other people, always fearing that they will be abandoned or mistreated yet again. This is not what God intended for them, but that they would be interdependent and emotionally satisfied in their relationships. Children deprived of the normal, loving, stable, family background will have more hurdles to face in adult life. It is no surprise to find that children in the UK. who have experienced such backgrounds and who have often been in multiple foster or care homes are far more likely to end up in criminal activities leading to imprisonment in later life.

It is therefore so wonderful when God places loving, caring people around such children, graciously granting them the chance to know human love and who also reflect the love of Jesus into their lives. This is what is happening through the Parental Care Ministries in Uganda and many children are finding the love of God which will last forever – for all time and eternity.

Chapter Two
EMMY'S STORY

"Don't eat it. Don't touch it!" Emmy's stepsister whispered to him, but with an urgency in her voice. Emmy looked at her. Why was she saying that? Was she just being mean to him again? He had no real fondness for this stepsister. She was not a blood relation, not the child of his father, but had been brought into the family when his father had taken another wife.

Emmy looked at his plate. He was a growing lad of fourteen and was starving. It was so unusual for his stepmother to even leave him any lunch. Perhaps his sister was jealous that her mother had thought of him. He was used to being used as a slave and was half-starved. He picked up his plate and was about to eat, when once again his sister spoke urgently to him in a quiet voice so that her mother would not hear.

"Don't touch it, Emmy; don't eat it!" she said, trying to stop Emmy from taking his plate. He pushed away her hand. Why would she stop him from having his lunch?

"Please leave me alone and let me eat" he said. "I'm so hungry!"

Then Emmy looked at her face and she seemed really serious, not just trying to be mean or unkind. Somehow he understood that she really didn't want him to eat the plate of food.

"What's the problem? Why shouldn't I eat my food?" he asked her. "When my mum was making the food she did it in secret. She was hiding, not wanting anyone to see what she was doing. She put something suspicious into it – I am really worried that there is something wrong with it – something in it to harm you. Please, please don't eat it Emmy!"

Emmy thought for a moment before he ate. Maybe something wasn't right. After all, his stepmother hated him, treated him badly and normally cleared all the food away before he came home so that he had to go without any lunch. It did seem strange that some had been left out for him. In spite of the rivalry between Emmy and his stepsister, she sounded genuine and really scared for him. Had his stepmother used some witchcraft to poison him? The practice of witchcraft was rife in Uganda, and it would not be unknown to consult a witch doctor to hurt someone in your extended family whom you did not love.

Emmy decided not to chance eating the food. He figured there was one way to know if it was poisoned. In the family compound was a pigsty. Emmy took the food which had been prepared for him and went behind the house to the sty and fed it to the pig. The following morning he went to look at the pig. To his immense shock, the pig was dead! Emmy then realised that the food had been deliberately poisoned and had he eaten it, he most likely would have been killed. Now, knowing his life was in danger, Emmy knew he had to think and act quickly. He needed to escape at once.

If he ran into the village or the surrounding area he would be recognised and be taken home again. He needed to get far away. If he could reach the capital city of Kampala with its crowded streets, then perhaps he would be safe. A truck transported bananas from the village to Kampala, leaving each evening. Emmy clambered on top of the bananas and sat there through the four-hour drive in darkness. He was very cold because he had no jacket to wear and it was the rainy season when the temperature falls considerably, especially at night.

It was a turning point in Emmy's life. His sad childhood was left behind – but he had no idea if his future would be any better. He just knew he had to flee from the evil designs of his stepmother.

What had caused things to be so bad for this young boy?

~

Emmanuel Nnyanzi had been born on Christmas Eve, 24th December 1968 in the village of Kalisizo in Rakai District, Uganda, into the Baganda tribe. His mother's name is Julian Nsabamukama. Emmy was her first child, but she was not a very happy wife or in a happy marriage. In fact, she was not the first wife of her husband, who was already fifty-nine years old, and considered to be an old man when they married. He already had around twelve wives, although some had separated and left the family. After Emmy's birth she bore him two further children, another son and a daughter. Emmy's parents had a lot of problems and challenges in their relationship. It didn't help that his father was drinking a lot of alcohol. There are several types of bananas which grow very well in the fertile soil of Uganda, and one type is used to brew banana beer. This beer is very potent and although it may temporarily cause people to forget their present problems, it soon brings further ones, such as abuse and addiction. Emmy's dad often had to be brought home by friends after a bout of drinking, as he was unable to walk by himself. Matters were made worse because Julian then began to drink, too, although she was still just a teenager. There were fights almost every night, and in the end his mum made the decision to run away and leave her husband. Already, Emmy's father had taken yet another wife who came into the marital home along with a child she already had.

~

Emmy was eight when his parents separated and his mother left home. That was the time when his life really took a turn for the worse. The new wife resented the three children who had been left behind and for whose care she was now responsible. Even though they were so young, she hated them and made them work like slaves. Emmy, as the eldest, suffered the most.

In the village there was no running water and so the children had to walk miles to collect water in containers and carry it all the way home. Then, as all cooking was done outside using three large stones to make a fireplace and burning wood, the children were sent daily to scour the countryside and find wood for burning, whatever the weather. Each house would have a small plot of land, called a 'shamba' – a garden. This was the only source of food for most families, and the children would be sent out to dig the plot, plant the seeds, weed the ground, water it all during the dry season and then harvest the results. If the rains failed to come, there would follow a drought and famine which meant very little food for the family. Emmy and his siblings would be the last on the list to be fed. Even though the stepmother's daughter was not the biological child of his dad, she was treated far better than Emmy and his brother and sister.

Although he worked so hard every single day, Emmy was never appreciated or thanked by his stepmother. In fact, whatever he did was met only by complaints and grumbling. The six years following his mother's desertion were terrible for Emmy. He had little to eat, usually only having a small portion of food in the evening. He had no one to comfort him or encourage him. Just when he thought that life could not get any worse, he found that his stepmother was trying to poison him! Thank God for the stepsister who had enough courage to tell Emmy that his food had been poisoned, and that his life was at risk. Little did she know, as she gave her warning, that not only was she saving one child's life, but that through him she would be the means of saving hundreds of others!

Chapter Three

LIFE BEGINS TO CHANGE FOR THE BETTER

Fleeing in fear and desperation from the only home he knew, to a totally unknown future was a terrifying situation for Emmy to find himself in on that cold Saturday night. When he arrived in Kampala he then had to somehow find his way to the home of a relative who he knew resided there. He roughly knew the area where his relative lived, but he did not have an exact address. Just a lad of fourteen with absolutely no possessions, money or clothes, other than those he was wearing, he was taken into the home of his relative.

This relative was not willing or able to look after Emmy and educate him as a son, but he did find him a job as a houseboy. The job of a houseboy in East Africa resembles in many ways the role of a 'maid of all work' in British homes during Victorian times. From early morning until late at night they were expected to clean the house, wash the dishes, do the laundry and ironing, fetch and carry for all the family members. It was menial work and the pay was poor, with few prospects for advancement. It was also very labour-intensive, as most homes did not have modern appliances like washing machines, and also in the hot and dusty climate the house needed cleaning each day.

Emmy wasn't given a room of his own; he had to sleep on the floor in the sitting room of the house, which meant he had to be the first up and the last to bed every day! It wasn't easy for him, for although he had done many chores in the village for his stepmother, he had never been in a house with electricity or water coming out of taps. It was all completely new and quite a culture shock for him. His employer, the mistress of the house, was not kind or understanding. This woman had no patience with the fourteen-year-old-boy who had come straight from the bush, even though he was willing to learn. Instead of teaching him, she expected him to do everything perfectly and to her liking. When he failed to do so, he was beaten and banged against a wall!

Even though Emmy had never set eyes on an electric iron before entering that house, he was expected to use one without being shown how it worked, and to iron all the family's clothes beautifully.

Emmy's employer had some children who were older than he was, so it seemed a good idea for him to ask their advice about how to use the iron. He did this and they were happy to show him, but when their mother saw them helping Emmy, she was furious!

"I didn't employ you so that my children would work for you, but so that you would work for them!" she shouted.

Emmy was made to feel very bad in that house – not like a child as her children were, not even like a human being with feelings or even basic human rights. He felt so rejected and depressed and wished that he had never been born. He had run away from the village because he had been unloved and abused and had hoped for a better life in Kampala, but in fact he had gone 'from the frying pan into the fire'.

Emmy knew that he couldn't stay in that environment and so made the decision to quit his job as a houseboy. He left and went to a cousin. His cousin was married to a builder who, at that time was engaged in several building projects. Emmy began working with him on the building sites, doing labouring jobs, such as carrying mixed concrete and loads of bricks to the masons who were using them, and long poles and timbers to the carpenters. This was another very tough job for such a young boy to do. He worked from early morning until late at night carrying bricks and sand in a wheelbarrow or in a pod on his head. The pay for such hard work was exceedingly poor and it was a struggle for Emmy who was by now fifteen or so years old. He was not a large, strong lad, probably partly because he had lived all his life only eating a poor and meagre diet. Indeed on this job he had to go without food all through the day and just had supper when he eventually arrived back at the house.

However, while working at the building site Emmy made a friend who frequently asked him about his schooling and if he was able to teach. Emmy had only completed primary school, but even so his new friend took him to the school where he was working and was able to get him a job there. Uganda at that time had a scheme for licensed teachers who have not been fully qualified. Emmy's friend lent him books about teaching and helped him to plan lessons. His sunny nature soon helped him to make other friends among the teaching staff and they, too, helped him with classroom skills and lesson preparation. A bright young man, he quickly learnt how to teach and at last had found a job he enjoyed! Through these skills God was preparing Emmy for his future life work, but, of course, he had no idea of that then! He had no idea either that God had also planned for him to meet his life partner at that school!

After about a year at the school he met and became friends with a young lady assistant teacher called Sarah.

One morning Sarah came to school looking very sad and this troubled Emmy.

"Why are you so unhappy?" he asked. "What is wrong?"

Sarah felt she could trust Emmy with her story.

"I live with my father and two stepmothers" she told him. "My stepmothers hate me so much and tell lies about me to my father, falsely accusing me. This has now caused a big rift between us."

Sarah's mother had also run away and separated from her husband when Sarah was very small, leaving her in the care of her father. This story, so similar to his own, touched his heart. It drew them close together and the friendship began to blossom into a deeper relationship as they understood each other's problems and were able to sympathise and share comfort. Although they were both only nineteen years old, they decided to get married on 29th January 1989. It was a civil wedding since at that time they did not know and love the Lord, although they were starting to attend a church. It was at an evangelistic mission in May 1989 that they both committed themselves to Jesus Christ. This was the turning point in their lives!

Chapter Four

GROWING IN THE CHRISTIAN
FAITH

Emmy and Sarah truly found love and friendship within God's family, bonding quickly with the pastor and the people. As a young married couple who had received very little love in their childhood or youth, it must have been wonderful to be welcomed with joy into the family of the church! Within the church there were many others who had experienced brokenness and suffering and who had also found healing and so knew how to love hurting people and help them to find God's healing, too.

Within this church Emmy and Sarah found a new peace and were enthusiastic about joining in many of the programmes which the church ran. Emmy became part of the team which engaged in house-to-house evangelism. He knew very little about how to communicate the gospel, but his heart was burning with the desire to pass on to others the wonderful news of Jesus Christ he had received and which had changed his life. Little by little, the leader of the house-to-house evangelism team took Emmy 'under his wing' and taught him how to reach others for Christ and how to preach the good news of the gospel. He learnt how to answer the questions people asked him and this evangelistic work thrilled his soul and created within him a burning passion to reach those without Christ and without hope. Soon this passion seemed to be moving him in a specific direction – a longing to return to his home village and share the gospel there.

The voice of the Holy Spirit within Emmy was so persistent that he went to talk things over with his pastor, Fred Sozi of the Soul Winning and Deliverance Church. He shared his calling to go back to his village to preach.

"If you hear that voice, please just obey God and do it, and the Lord will be with you" his wise pastor told him. Pastor Fred prayed with him and released him for this new ministry.

~

Living in the capital city of Kampala was not easy, and Emmy had struggled financially to support his family, for by this time he and Sarah were the proud parents of two daughters, Grace and Faith. So Emmy sent his wife and children back to the village while he stayed in Kampala looking for a job in order to provide for them, with the view of joining them at a later date to work as an evangelist. At the time it seemed the sensible thing to do, because after leaving Pastor Fred's office that day with his blessing to return to the village, Emmy bumped into the church elder.

"Brother, you are just the man I was looking for!" he exclaimed. "I have a job for you at my school!" Emmy was delighted to be offered this position and started once more to teach. It seemed to be God's provision. Soon he forgot all about his calling to return to the village and preach. The elder was delighted with Emmy's work, so much so that he made him his deputy when he needed to be out of his office! However, there was a definite down side to this arrangement. The elder paid his other teachers their salaries, but not Emmy.

"Brother, I'm sure you don't mind" he said to Emmy, "Allow me to pay these teachers and as soon as I have enough money then I'll pay you."

Emmy agreed at first, but after eight months without pay, he felt something had to be done, for his dear wife and children were suffering back in the village. They were living in a very small mud hut and only had the food which they managed to grow in their garden. They had no money at all. He badly needed those wages! Things were so bad that one day Emmy felt he had to share with Pastor Fred the way in which the elder was treating him. He thought that perhaps the pastor would speak to the elder and tell him to put things right.

Emmy broke down into tears as he told his story to Pastor Fred. He expected the pastor to be indignant at the injustice of it all. However, Pastor Fred was silent for a while, then shocked Emmy with his reply.

"I feel the Holy Spirit is telling me to say to you that you are more rebellious than Jonah"

This was not the answer Emmy had expected! He thought that the pastor would go at once to the elder and at least question him as to why he wasn't paying Emmy! He was indignant to be told he was rebellious, but also very confused and didn't make any reply to Pastor Fred. His pastor looked at him and asked another question, "I remember a little while ago you came here and told me that the Holy Spirit had told you to go and preach in your home village." Emmy nodded his head in agreement and answered 'Yes'.

"Then why didn't you go?"

Emmy had no answer to that question. Inwardly he made a promise to the Lord that as soon as he had enough money for the bus fare home, he would go and obey the call to preach in the village.

One evening soon after giving this promise to the Lord, Emmy had just returned to the place where he was lodging, when one of the church members came to his door. This lady had no idea of Emmy's situation or needs, but she came with a gift.

"I felt that the Lord was telling me to give you this gift," she commented as she handed him some money. It was just the correct number of shillings for Emmy's fare back to his home village! How Emmy praised God for this gift and His timing! However, it was only enough for the bus fare. There was nothing left over for a gift for Sarah or his two little girls, Grace and Faith. How he would have loved to have given them just a small gift each! He went back on the bus, crying because he had no idea what he was going to do next. He had no income, no job prospects and felt he was such a useless husband and father.

Emmy's home village was called Kyasenya. When he arrived he was so depressed and felt so ashamed that at first he wouldn't leave the house and walk in the village or talk to people. Emmy describes his feelings like those of Naomi when she returned from Moab to Bethlehem. Naomi and her family had left Bethlehem (which means the 'House of Bread') in a time of famine and gone to the country of Moab. There her boys married foreign wives and then her husband and both of her sons died. One day she heard there was food again in Bethlehem and obeyed God's call to return. Her daughter-in-law, Ruth, went with her, but they returned with nothing. Naomi begged the townspeople to call her 'Mara'-meaning 'bitterness,' for she had left in hope and fullness and returned empty.

Emmy had not lost his family as Naomi had, but he had returned with nothing. He had absolutely nothing, whereas those friends and relatives left behind when he went to Kampala, had thrived and owned much more than he did.

Both Emmy and Sarah had to come to the point where they could truly forgive their families for all the hurt they had received as children. They knew they would not be able to minister to them or love them as they ought, unless they were able to forgive them. This was not an easy thing to do, but studying the story of Joseph and his brothers in the book of Genesis helped them to come to the point where they could forgive their relatives and truly mean what they said. Together they made a vow to the Lord that they would forgive everyone who had hurt them and caused them pain. Emmy's determination was: "Before I meet them again, I say now that I will never speak anything to them reminding them of what they did to me. But what I am going to do is this; I am going to do actions which will show them that I am a changed person and that I love them."

This victory over hate and bitterness, and the vow to forgive, moulded this young couple (or rather, allowed the Master Potter to remould and remake them) so that they could radiate God's love to all they met. It has been a powerful testimony which has melted many hardened hearts!

~

After a few days of much introspection, Emmy plucked up the courage to get out and about in the village. Gradually his confidence grew and he was able to share Jesus with the people he met as he walked around. In due course he, along with Pastor Kwizera, were able to start the first church in Kanoni village. The calling which God had given him to share the gospel in his own area was beginning to bear fruit. After a while the local church recognised Emmy's gifts and calling and he, along with Sarah and the two girls, and another pastor called Azalia Mugizi were sent by the church to minister in a different area. They became missionaries to people from another language group in the southwest of Uganda. They began work in the small town of Ishongororo. There, they joined with another pastor, Boaz Karuhanga, and as a team began to preach the gospel in the town and surrounding villages. It was by no means easy because these missionaries had to learn the local language of Runyankole, for they spoke the Luganda language. It took them some while to become fluent in the new language.

In Ishongororo one of the new converts was called Rose Munyosi. She actually lived in the town of Mbarara, but her husband, Martin, was a policeman and had been transferred to work at Ishongororo, leaving his wife, and their children still living in Mbarara. One day Rose, along with the children, had come to visit her husband and she found that there was a gospel crusade meeting being held close to the Ishongororo Police Station. On hearing the gospel preached, she and the three eldest of the children were saved and then later were baptized. They attended the church and meetings in Ishongororo for about two months, growing in the Lord. One day Rose told Emmy that it was time for her to return to Mbarara. He encouraged her to find a church there and continue to learn of the Lord. He also shared his dream that the time would come when they would also plant a church in Mbarara.

Rose's response to this was to tell Pastor Emmy that her prayer was that they would plant the church at once so that she could continue to worship with them. She owned a small house in the town, and promised to ask her husband's permission to allow it to be used for church services. Although Martin had not become a Christian, he readily agreed and so the church began in Mbarara with eight women and children, and Emmy as their pastor. The group worshipped together in the open space of the compound of her small mud house. Some old canvas, which had many holes was spread over the compound in order to bring a little shelter from the elements. Neighbours kindly lent chairs, so that the congregation could sit down for the service, and everyone collected them before it began and returned them afterwards. The small group worshipped the Lord with all their hearts and every day they went around the neighbourhood, visiting people in their homes and sharing the good news of Jesus. Many people responded to the gospel and gave their hearts to the Lord and also many were healed through prayer. With these wonderful results the group were encouraged to keep on preaching.

It was while preaching in this community that the need for parental care became evident. One of the original eight members of the church which met in Rose's home became sick and died. Her husband suffered from severe mental illness and was unable to care for his children. The husband, being a Moslem, had named the three children Falidah, Aisha and Imamu. These children were crying day and night in their distress. It touched the hearts of Pastor Emmy and Sarah so much to see the desperate situation in which these children found themselves, and they began to pray for them.

One day, while in prayer, Emmy heard the inner voice whisper to him, "Faith without actions is dead. Be the one to feed these children."

In fact, Pastor Emmy and Sarah were very poor and barely managed to feed their own family, which had grown by now to two girls and two boys, Grace, Faith, Daniel and Roger. They lived together in one single rented room, but they took these extra three children to live with them. As they lived together they came to realise that it wasn't material things which these children needed, but parental love. The children began to replace their tears with smiles and they put smiles on the faces of Emmy and Sarah, too, as they saw their happiness. At this time the family expanded once again to take in another little girl called Mariam, whose father had died. From this tiny beginning, the work has grown to care for over 2,000 children in seven schools; a home for needy babies and more than seventy children who actually live in Emmy and Sarah's own home. Also seventy-four churches have been planted, of which Pastor Emmy is the overseer, and a gospel radio station has been established.

Chapter Five

THE STORY OF A MOTHER'S TORMENT

It is hard for those of us who live in the developed world to understand what life was like for the majority of the population of rural Uganda, or indeed, in many other countries of Africa, just a couple of generations ago. Uganda has been catapulted into this technological age within the last decade or so. Now, use of mobile phones and access to the Internet is possible almost anywhere, but for Emmy's mother, growing up, life was a different scenario.

When Julian Nsabamukama was born, it was into a family which had not had the opportunity of any formal education. Because her parents had not been to school, they certainly saw no reason why they should send their daughter to one. As was the normal procedure in Uganda at that time, Julian was born at home, in the small mud house, with no medical help available. As she grew up, she asked which day was her birthday, but she was not told, simply because her parents couldn't remember the date. Her birth wasn't registered. Her babyhood was spent strapped to her mother's back with a cloth – a warm and comforting place for an infant. Wherever mother went, to the shamba (garden) to hoe or to harvest; to the village market to buy supplies; or outside the house cooking the meals, Julian went with her. Later she would toddle around the compound, gradually learning to help with the chores by watching her mother and siblings. When she became eight she began her work as a cowherd, looking after her parents' cattle. She took the cattle into the bush, moving with them from place to place as they found new pasture. This was an important and responsible job, because cattle are very precious and they are the wealth of the family. This was Julian's work for the next eight years, until she was sixteen and considered to be grown up and of marriageable age.

Sometime when she was sixteen or seventeen her parents called her indoors for a discussion.

"You are now a grown-up and can be married. There is a man who is interested in taking you as his wife. He will soon come to see you," her parents told her.

Very shortly after this conversation her parents announced to her one day,

"There is no need for you to take the cows to the bush tomorrow. Someone else will take them out because we have visitors arriving. These are your visitors. The man we told you about is coming to visit with you."

It wasn't good news for Julian. She was very scared and started crying. Her weeping continued through the day. There was no way she felt ready to be sent away to another family and be married. She was a shy young lady and just wanted to stay near the friends with whom she had grown up in the village and played with all her life.

When the visitors arrived, Julian hid in the back room of the house as soon as she heard her parents welcoming the guests into the sitting room. Her heart began to thump wildly in her chest. Julian then ran outside the house and hid behind it, dreading meeting this stranger. Her mother found her there, crying her heart out. She tried to calm Julian and reassure her that all would be well. After all, wasn't marriage the normal thing for all young girls? Eventually she persuaded Julian to go into the house and greet the visitors and meet the man whom she was to marry.

Had Julian hoped to see some handsome young beau? I guess she hoped so but in fact she was horrified when she saw a man who was about as old as her father! However, as a daughter, she had no say in the matter. It was all arranged and she had to marry him. Just a girl herself, she was very afraid of this man, and for about a month she refused to allow him into her bedroom.

Her husband already had one wife, who was around the age of her own mother and had now reached the time when she could no longer become pregnant. That was why he wanted to marry a young girl who he hoped would produce many more children for him. Julian was very fortunate in that the first wife not only accepted her presence but was also very kind to her and treated her like a daughter. She counselled her and told her not to be afraid, but to allow her husband his marital rights.

After a month of marriage, Julian's childhood friends came to pay her a visit. It was such a joy to her and they played together. She felt happy in the way she had felt in her parents' home. When they left, she was plunged back into sadness and despondency. She cried so much because she had longed to return home with them, but of course, that wasn't possible.

Because Julian had no choice in the marriage process, she had no love for her husband and there was a lot of arguing and strife within the relationship. There was such a huge gap between their ages and they had nothing in common.

In due course Julian became pregnant and gave birth to Emmy. Not being sure of her actual age, Julian thinks she was possibly eighteen by that time. Two years later a little girl was born to the couple and another son, two years after that, but things within the marriage did not improve. Julian's husband was often drunk and she also began to drink, so the quarrels were frequent and fierce. Before long her husband decided to take a third wife – and when this happened she left him and went her own way.

This was a very difficult decision for Julian to make. She virtually had no options, because she didn't know where she would go and had no home to offer the children. The two younger children didn't have quite such a bad time as Emmy He took the brunt of his new stepmother's hatred since he was the eldest.

Eventually Julian remarried and gave birth to another three children, but sadly, only one of them survived. In time her second husband died, too, but this was after Emmy and Sarah had married, and also after he had become a born again Christian. He knew then that he had a responsibility to forgive his mother for abandoning her children.

When Emmy and Sarah returned to the village to begin preaching, they found Emmy's father was now living alone, as the stepmother had also left him. They were reconciled with him and Emmy felt it was the time to try and reconcile his mother to his father. Julian then returned and lived with her husband until he died, although it continued to be a very stormy relationship.

At the end of her husband's life, when he was very sick, Julian called for Emmy and Sarah to come. Emmy had the opportunity to share the gospel once again, and this time his dad responded and repented, and in spite of his weakness was able to repeat a prayer after Emmy, accepting the Lord into his life. Two days later he peacefully slipped into a coma and died.

After Emmy's father died, his mother continued for a while to live on her own in the village. She was still addicted to alcohol and this made her weak and she fell sick several times. About eight years ago Emmy went to visit her and found her alone in her house, a very sick woman, so he asked her to come and live with him and Sarah. She was very happy to do so and they took good care of her, nursing her back to health. She has stayed with them ever since and is a happy mother and grandmother, blessing others with her love and care. She accepted Jesus as her Saviour and is now fulfilled in a life of thankful service to her beloved Lord. God has restored to her 'the years which the locusts have eaten' (Joel 2:25 NIV).

Chapter Six

THE EARLY DAYS AND BIRTH OF
PARENTAL CARE MINISTRIES

When Emmy and Sarah had been commissioned and sent to the Ankole district of Uganda from the Baganda district of Uganda, their task was to preach the gospel of the saving grace of Jesus and to plant churches. To begin with, they lived in the town of Ishongororo and worked faithfully together with the other two pastors, fulfilling this commission in an amazing way. Through their preaching of the truth of God, many people were saved and little churches began to spring up all over the district. The people were poor, living very simply, as did Emmy, Sarah and their growing family. The churches were mostly mud-brick structures, with holes for windows and no doors, covered by corrugated iron sheet roofs. Emmy and Sarah walked miles to reach and encourage the small churches and Emmy had a burden for the new believers to be taught in the faith and to see young leaders grow in their knowledge of the Bible. He recognised the need for them to have regular teaching, so after Emmy had moved his family from Ishongororo to Mbarara, and the work developed further, he was able to establish the 'Ezra School of Ministry.' This gave men and women the opportunity to come to Mbarara and study through the school holidays. The church had already started a small primary school in a mud-brick church on the outskirts of Mbarara, and during the long school holidays the building was used as the

Bible school and was a great blessing to the young pastors who were looking after the growing number of village churches.

The Ezra School of Ministry still continues, but has been relocated to the new Parental Care Senior School, where there is a conference room.

The original church which had started in Rose's house soon grew too large and a larger meeting place was needed, so they rented a downtown, incomplete house for use as a church building. The local stork and vulture population must have wanted to join in the worship because they frequented the tin roof, marching up and down and making a lot of noise! The building was far from ideal, situated near the town rubbish tip! At that time the church was called, "The Saints' Gate Pentecostal Church." When I first visited in 2002 it was full of worshippers who joyfully praised the Lord in spite of all the inconveniences. It was a wonderful experience to join with people who were so poor in the eyes of the world, but so very rich in faith! I was humbled and privileged to share in their worship.

Already, both Emmy and Sarah had a deep concern for children who were living in bad situations and circumstances. First, there had been the four abandoned children who joined their family, then two children from Ishongororo had been 'given' to them by their dying mother. She had become a believer, but as their father was a drunkard and not able to care for them, she was concerned for their future. Although they remained in schools in Ishongororo, Emmy was responsible for their school fees and well-being and they lived with his family during the holidays. Soon a pattern began to develop where children in need of love and care were accepted into the family. These children were treated in exactly the same way as their own biological children were – they lived together happily as brothers and sisters.

Later in 2002, after the money had been provided for a good house for the Nnyanzi family, the number of children began to increase, for both Emmy and Sarah could not refuse to care for children in need of parental love. Their own experiences had left such a deep imprint on their lives that neither of them wanted to see other children suffer in the same way.

When I was a young woman I was given a book to read. It was entitled, *Don't Waste Your Sorrows*. Certainly Emmy and Sarah did not waste the sorrows they endured as children! This challenged me, too, because I at that time still held bitterness towards some of my family because of abuse which I had suffered in childhood. I knew that I had to deal with the issue and offer forgiveness freely and fully even as I had received forgiveness from the Lord and He had given me healing.

Over the next few years when I went to Mbarara to visit, the family kept growing and it was becoming very difficult for Emmy and Sarah to provide for the children. School fees were a problem, especially for the children attending senior school. I tried to find sponsors among my friends in England for as many as possible, but it was obvious that another solution had to be found. Sarah had started a primary school in Ishongororo and loved teaching, so began to use a small mud-brick church building on a site a little way out of the main town. It had some benches on the mud floor, but no teaching aids at all. However, it was a start. The school was initially called The Henderson School, after Hugh Henderson who had been such a helper and encourager to Emmy. An adjoining plot of land became available for £500. It seemed to be an amazing provision to extend the school, so I told my church family the Sunday morning after I had heard about it and before I left the service, people had pledged the whole amount!!

In 2006 I was able to take a small team over to Mbarara which included another Emmi – a Romanian lad who had become like a son to me. He had recently married, and both he and his wife, Kerin, also had hearts full of love and concern for children. After working on various projects for three weeks, during the fourth week, along with Pastor Emmy, in the old minibus with Emmy D, the driver, we all went to Kenya to visit an orphanage called Kanyawegi by the side of Lake Victoria in the town of Kisumu. It was an interesting trip for us all and Emmy found it helpful to see how the Lord was working in that situation and he was able to talk through issues with the people there.

I remember telling Pastor Emmy the story of George Muller (1805-1898) who founded the Muller Homes on Ashley Down in Bristol in the nineteenth century and the wonderful ways in which God provided for those children. George Muller lived by faith, only talking to God, his loving Father, about their needs.

When I was around ten years old I was taken on a visit to see the homes that were under Muller's care. Only a few children were living there then because most were being housed in small family units. However, learning the story of this great man of faith moved me deeply even though I was not a Christian at that time. George Muller's childhood could not have been more different from that of Emmy and Sarah. Born into the family of a comparatively wealthy Prussian tax collector, he not only enjoyed having everything he needed, including an excellent education, but he was also his father's favourite son. Yet, in spite of generous allowances, even as a child he frequently stole from his father and habitually lied. In his youth his father chose his career path and set him on the way to becoming a Lutheran minister, which was a well-paid career in those days in Germany. Yet George had no personal faith and loved 'wine, women and song' as the saying goes. His life became seriously out of control and by the time he was sixteen he landed up in gaol! Eventually he went back to school and studied well, being a very clever lad, but still spent money extravagantly, gambled a great deal and incurred huge debts, even as he prepared to go to Halle University to study theology. While at university he started to go to some Christian meetings and there the Lord met with him and he found forgiveness for his sins and new life in Jesus. His fellow students were amazed to witness the transformation in his life. In 1826, he began to read about missionary work and felt God calling him to serve in this way.

His father was very angry and implored his son not to take this path, and if he persisted in doing so, he would no longer be called his son. Because of this George felt he could no longer accept the generous allowance from his father as he would no longer be studying to become the well-paid minister his father had wanted him to be, so he began his life of faith, trusting God to supply all his needs. The Lord did not let his child down and through the kindly interest of one of his professors, he was given work, which paid enough for his needs.

Near the university was an orphanage which had been established centuries before by one of the university professors, in order, primarily, to care for poor children in the area, but also to house poor students. George qualified for a place there, living among the 2000 bright and happy children whose home it was.

After graduating, George came to London in order to train with the London Missionary Society, hoping in time to work among Jewish people. This is when he learnt to speak English. He also began to read the Bible in a new way and understand about the Holy Spirit's longing to fill his life. He was no longer just studying in an academic way, but listening for the Lord to speak personally to him. This led to him becoming the pastor of Ebenezer Chapel at Teignmouth in Devon. It was there that he met and married his wife, Mary. Together they lived, believing God's promises that He would supply all their needs. In 1832 the couple moved to minister in Bristol. They planted several small churches as well as pastoring their own. Soon afterwards there was a terrible cholera epidemic which ravaged the area of Bristol in which they were living – and it pained George and Mary to see so many starving, orphaned children in the streets around them. They began to feed them from their home and also to try to hold some classes to educate them, as they did not attend school.

The couple supported both Sunday schools and day schools, where all the teachers were Christians, gave out Bibles, supported missionary work, and founded along with a great friend, 'Scriptural Knowledge Institution for Home and Abroad'.

In 1835 George Muller was one day thinking back to his days when he was staying at the orphanage in Halle, and, as he thought about the children there, he felt the Holy Spirit leading him to trust the Lord to build an 'orphan House' in Bristol. There was no orphanage in Bristol at that time. Orphans were sent to the workhouses, which had a dreadful reputation for unkindness and even cruelty towards the inmates.

George and Mary began to pray and donations began to pour in, and people even began to offer their services to work with the children.

In December 1835 George had prayed to the Lord and asked for buildings and staff and £1,000 to start an orphanage – a prayer of faith for what amounted to a huge amount in those days. In June 1837, the last of that amount had been provided! By that time two homes had been built, one for boys and one for girls.

Through these years, George often suffered from ill health, and yet still the work grew and grew. How that reminds me of the early days when Emmy and Sarah began to care for orphans and needy children in Mbarara – when Emmy also had sickness to deal with as well and constant challenges from health issues within his own family, and his prayerful dependence for God to supply all their needs.

In August 1838 George wrote in his diary that 'I have not one penny in hand for the orphans; in a day or two many pounds will be needed.' On that very day, before evening, a woman who knew nothing of the needs stopped by and gave £5.00 for the children! Two days later the money had run out and again George prayed. A lady whom he had never met, but who was staying in Clifton heard of the work and sent £12! God is so faithful! This kind of story was repeated over and over again.

My favourite story of God's provision for the orphans I heard on my visit to the orphanage when I was ten years old. I remember retelling it to Pastor Emmy when we were going to Kanyawegi orphanage in Kenya.

On one occasion all the children were sitting at the table waiting for breakfast, but there was no food in the kitchen for them. As usual they gave thanks, and looked up expectantly. The doorbell clanged loudly and George Muller opened it. Outside was the baker.

"My cart has just broken" he said, "It is full of bread. Can you make use of it because it will take all day for the cart to be repaired?"

Could they use it! It was heaven-sent and all the children ate fresh bread that had been baked that very morning!

Eventually five large purpose-built homes were built on Ashley Down to house the growing number of children who now came from all over Britain. Many were children who were living on the streets in the country's ports and were very vulnerable. These buildings were not just homes, they were schools, too. The children wore a uniform and were also taught about the loving heavenly Father who longed to have them in His family. They learnt to pray and many, many of them grew up to be committed Christians. When they reached adulthood, the Mullers' Homes helped to teach the young people a trade and then place them in a safe working environment. People in the area commented on how much the Muller family really loved each child, even though there were so many of them as the work grew.

~

I have included this story of George Muller in this book because in many ways Pastor Emmy and Sarah are following in his footsteps. As more and more children came into their extended family, so boarding houses were added to the schools. The children were given uniforms, taught academic subjects, as well as how much God loves them and wants to be their Father, and they learnt to pray. Even as more and more children have joined the 'family,' so God has provided for building after building, for food on the table and clothes and shoes and school supplies! What a wonderful God who responds when we trust Him to provide all our needs.

~

A few years after the work with the children began to grow and the first school was established, Emmy knew that he needed to register the school and work with the Ugandan government as an NGO. (Non-governmental Organisation). It took a lot of work to have a document drawn up which would satisfy the government. At first Emmy and Sarah, along with their colleagues, Pastor Charles and his wife, Grace, myself and Hugh Henderson were named on the document as trustees. However, Hugh and I were not at that time in a position to undertake being trustees, so the document was rewritten. God had other partners waiting in the wings! The new ministry was called, 'Parental Care Ministries' and the name of the school was changed to reflect this new title. In an amazing answer to prayer the document was accepted and passed by the Ugandan authorities.

Parental Care Ministries had been born!

Chapter Seven
PASTOR CHARLES'S STORY

Charles Ochwo was born on 2nd April 1967, and like Emmy and Sarah, he, too, had an unhappy family life. Charles and his brother were deserted by their mother, who separated from his father when they were just little boys. Then they were taken into the homes of various stepmothers. In fact, their father married more than twenty women, so there was no stability within the home. Charles was a bright lad and completed primary school education followed by the first two years of secondary school. He then quit school because his father was mistreating him so much that he decided he must leave home and begin a fresh life on his own.

In 1991 he married Grace, whom he had met during the time when he was at secondary school. She had been attending the local primary school.

In 1992 their first child, Isaac, was born. It was around this time that Charles began to drink heavily and this became a persistent problem in his life. Three years later he left the area where they were living, going to Kampala, hoping to work in the building industry. In Kampala Charles managed to find a job with the ROKO Construction Company. However, in 1997, after only two years of working for them, the company acquired the contract to build the Bank of Uganda branch in Mbarara, so Charles was sent to work there. All through this time his problem with drink continued and this brought a negative impact on all his lifestyle.

One day in August 1998 he was due to meet up with a workmate and go on a drinking binge, but while his friend was looking for somewhere where they might sit, Charles found a leaflet, which he picked up and read. It was a tract – a message from the Bible telling the story of the Rich Fool in Luke 12:13-21. This story spoke so deeply into his heart that instead of staying with his friend and getting drunk, he decided to return home. This became a turning point in his life.

The following Sunday Charles took his two sons along with him to a local church. It was the Saint's Gate Church in Mbarara which had been planted by Pastor Emmy. Emmy wasn't there, for he was studying in New Zealand at that time, so the service was being conducted by some of the women. However that didn't put Charles off and he continued to attend each week. When Pastor Emmy returned and met him, he had a conviction in his spirit that the Lord was bringing this man into the fold and that he would become a co-worker. Meanwhile, Charles's heart was touched by the Lord and understood the gospel message, committing his life to Christ. Charles then went to tell Emmy the wonderful news that he had been saved.

"I believe that God is calling you to work with me in the ministry" was Emmy's response.

"How can that be?" asked Charles. "I have a family to support and I need to work".

"God has a good plan for your life and that of your family" answered Emmy. "Go home and read the Bible, pray and fast and the Lord will show you the answer".

Charles went home and did just that. As he read the Scriptures, he came to the verses in Jeremiah 42:7-17. God spoke to him through these verses.

He heard the Holy Spirit telling him, "My son, be faithful and serve me – all that you want is in the story." He understood that if he put the Lord first in his life and served Him, then the Lord would take care of him and his family.

Charles once again went to Emmy and shared what he had heard from the Lord. Emmy encouraged him and gave him this Scripture from Hebrews 6:9-10: "Even though we speak like this, dear friends, we are confident of better things in your case – things that accompany salvation. God is not unjust; he will not forget your work and the love you have shown him as you have helped his people and continue to help them" (NIV).

These words encouraged Charles to be confident that God would take care of him and help him to join Emmy in the ministry at the church, which was already beginning to expand into the Parental Care Ministry. In time he became a pastor.

Those early days were hard for Charles, Grace and the children. They needed about 1,000 Ugandan shillings a week in order to survive. Where would that money come from? It was a hard test of faith for such a young Christian to walk by faith and trust the Lord to supply all the material needs of the family.

God is always faithful to His children who trust Him. On December 26th 2001 Isaac, Charles's eldest son, had a dream. In that dream he saw his father and himself walking on water and going to the town centre of Mbarara.

That Christmas Charles had not been able to get the money he needed to buy meat. However, in faith he 'walked on the water' into the town and a Muslim woman gave him 1,000 shillings, so he was able to go to the slaughterhouse and buy a cow's lung for their Christmas feast. This miracle was a witness to Charles that the Lord would indeed provide for his family.

Charles and Grace and the children were living in a small mud-brick house of around 8 feet square. It was hard for them all. The children were not able to attend school, for there was no money to send them. They were the laughing stock of the area. People taunted them and said that Charles must have murdered someone in his home and that was why they were living in such bad circumstances! (It was

2002 before Isaac and his sister Doreen were able to start school, and by then Isaac was twelve!) In fact, in 2000 when their fourth child was born, Charles's brother came to visit and was appalled to see how the family were living and returned home to tell everyone about it and reported that his brother was a madman. Relationships with Grace's parents then deteriorated, too, as they heard the rumours.

Later in 2000 a policeman who owned a banana plantation in the village of Katete was transferred to work in another town and asked Charles to take care of the plantation for him and promised that he would pay 10,000 shillings a month for this work and also pay the rent on his small house. Charles worked faithfully for a year and a half, but no salary or rent was ever paid. However, Charles and Grace continued to trust the Lord and serve Him alongside Pastor Emmy in spite of all the difficulties.

I visited Mbarara in 2004 and this dear family opened their home and welcomed me with tea and home-grown peanuts. I was humbled at their generosity to share when they had so very little. On that visit I was doing a little cross-stitch – small pictures and Scriptures to put on greeting cards and sell to raise money to help the orphans. Charles and Isaac were fascinated and wanted to learn how to embroider. They quickly mastered the technique so I gave them all the supplies I had with me. Sometimes I would get up in the morning and see them outside in the old minibus sewing away!

I took their sewing home with me, made cards, and the proceeds were sent back to help the family. Somehow I managed to continue to supply them with canvas and threads. I spoke one afternoon at a Mothers' Union meeting in Chipping Sodbury and the ladies there, on hearing about Charles, Grace and their family, not only bought my entire stock of cards but also collected embroidery silks and sent them to me for Charles and Isaac.

The family continued to live in the small house until 2009. As Charles and Grace and their family were learning to live by faith, so the Lord was also teaching me to pray in faith for their needs and I also saw miracles happen, as people gave to help them.

The family continued to grow, and Mary Blessing was born on February 2nd 2006, the very day on which I flew back to England, having taken a team of young people from UK and Romania to serve in the church for a month. This daughter has indeed been a great blessing to the family, bringing them so much joy as she has grown up.

Charles and Grace had a great blow in April 2007. Charles became very, very sick. Some of his former life had caught up with him and he was diagnosed with AIDS and TB. His recovery was slow and he was instructed not to go to work. How would his family of seven be clothed and fed if he could no longer be active in the ministry or do other small jobs to supplement his income? It was a great test of faith for them all. He was given anti-retroviral drugs, which are very powerful in helping keep the AIDS virus under control, but the person taking them becomes extremely hungry and needs extra food. How grateful we are to the Lord that at that time the small bank account which I had opened to help projects such as PCM contained enough money to send some relief so that they could get a home of their own or buy land to build one in due course. Charles bought a plot of land, but was unable to start building.

Later that year, in July 2007, once again Charles fell very sick. He was so sick with meningitis that after a month of lying unconscious in the hospital his parents arrived, demanding to take him back to their village home so that he could die there. Pastor Emmy counselled his distraught wife, Grace, not to allow this to happen. So she refused to allow his parents to remove him. They left in anger and never returned. They did not even leave a small gift to help this struggling family.

But God is a faithful God and we can trust Him to provide for our needs when we are living in the centre of His will! Charles recovered from his meningitis without any residual side effects – truly another miracle of God's grace!

In April 2009 the family who owned the house where they were living decided to sell it and Charles's family were given eviction orders. They had no home into which they could move, but the Lord provided for them and the family had a new start in a new house! Once settled, the family began to learn a new skill, one which Charles could help with, since it wasn't strenuous – they began to make beads from paper and thread them into beautiful necklaces, which are sold in U.K. by PCM. This supplements the income and provides for the family.

July 2009 was also a very special time. Charles and Grace had only had a civil wedding, never having been able to afford a church wedding since their conversion. On July 27th Emmy had a very special wedding day for the couples in the church who had not been married in church, and Charles and Grace were part of that group. There was much rejoicing as vows were renewed before the Lord and marriages blessed!

Exactly two years later (in 2011) Charles was able to lay the foundation for his own house on the plot of land he had bought in 2007.

All through these difficult years Charles has been a faithful 'right hand man' to Emmy – he and Grace being partners and fully committed to the work of PCM. Their children have also been to the PCM school, which is a blessing not only to the orphaned children in the area, but also to the children of many pastors who would otherwise struggle to pay for their education.

Grace's Story

Charles's wife, Grace, also has her own sad childhood story. It is so amazing how God has redeemed the terrible sadness experienced in childhood of the four Ugandan trustees!

Grace's mother was still in Primary 7 when she became the girlfriend of an older man. He was already married with two wives and when he knew his girlfriend was pregnant he asked her parents if he could marry her, too. However, Grace's grandmother refused, not wanting her daughter to become a third wife – to have a life pretty much as a slave. Grace's mother was eighteen-years-old and she left school and stayed at home with her parents. Grace was born and her mother looked after her. She was an active baby, never even going through the crawling stage but walking at 8 -9 months! When Grace was two, her mother married another man and left her daughter in the care of her grandmother. Her mother showed no further love for her child, refusing even to buy her clothes, and when she came to visit she often hit Grace. She wouldn't allow Grace to call her 'mum', but made her call her 'aunt.' Grace's grandmother had several other granddaughters and grandsons, but Grace was always her favourite.

When Grace was about eight years old she was taken to Gulu to the home of a male cousin, where she was to work as a babysitter. She stayed there for three years before returning to her grandmother's home and resumed schooling once again in Primary 4.

There were rumours flying around about Grace's parentage and she learnt she was the daughter of Mr Stephen. His sister came to tell her that she was her aunt and was part of their family. It was shortly after this that Grace's dear grandmother died. Then she was really bereft. Her father's family took her into their home and her stepmother began to treat her very badly. Grace passed her final primary 7 examination, but was not allowed to continue her studies in secondary school. She was told that she had to look after her stepmother's children and would be taught to be a dressmaker. It was around that time that she met and married Charles – and the rest is history!

Pastor Emmanuel Nnyanzi and 'supermum' Sarah

Faith, Emmy and Sarah's second daughter

Pastor Emmy's mother, Julian

'Supermom' Sarah

Pastor Charles and Grace

*Pastor Emmy's eldest daughter, Grace, whose
story is included in the book*

Esther

Sarah and Emmy's youngest daughter,
Marie Julie

*Sarah with her two sons, Roger and Daniel and
their sister, Grace*

*Team of January 2006 from UK, Romania,
Rwanda and Uganda working with Pastor
Emmy for a month*

*Children in the Mbarara primary school – the
first PCM school to be established*

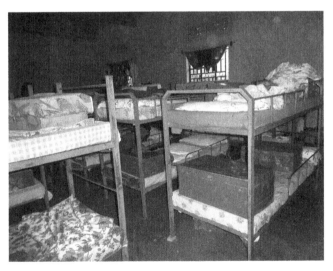

A dormitory at the first PCM primary school

Playtime at the Mbarara primary school

Church service under tarpaulin before the church was built

The new church building at Mbarara

Nigel Whitaker with children from Katyazo Senior School

Children at Kyhimba School who are in Primary Seven, ready to graduate to the Senior school

Buildings at Kyhimba School

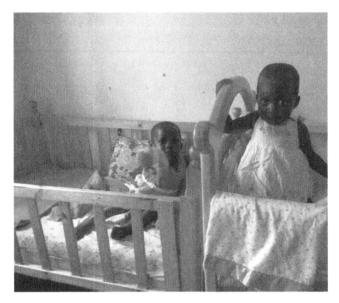

Children in the new baby home

Nursery nurse in the babies' home

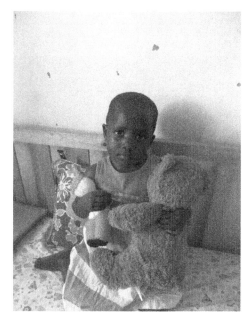

One of the children living in the new babies' home

Children at the Senior School at Katyazo

Senior pupils singing and dancing at Katyazo School

Students at Katyazo School

Happy children in one of the PCM schools

Working with the joyful children in one of the PCM schools

Children in the first school which was built at Mbarara

The gift of a goat to a needy family

Chapter Eight

THE WELSH PARTNERSHIP

Once Parental Care Ministries was established as a Ugandan NGO, the Lord began to work so that Emmy and Sarah had overseas partners who could help with finding sponsors for the children and join in praying for all the many needs and in turn be blessed by the prayers and love of the Ugandan children and workers. This has never been a one-way 'hand out' or even 'hand up,' but always a two-way enriching and blessed experience – a real partnership.

In 2006 when Laura Whitaker went on her own, at just sixteen years of age, to spend four weeks in Uganda, no one could have imagined how that visit would impact the friends in her church in Wales and grow into PCM UK.

The chaplain of St. David's College, Llandudno, had contacts in Uganda, and he arranged for some students to visit and experience the culture there. It was arranged for Laura to visit four locations, staying one week in each and living with local families. One of these weeks was in Mbarara with the Nnyanzi family. That week, living with Emmy and Sarah, made such a deep impression on Laura, that when she returned home, she spoke of this time as the highlight of the visit. Shortly after, when Pastor Emmy and his daughter Grace were in the UK, Laura's parents, Nigel and Marian, invited them for a meal to thank them for their care of Laura. They invited anyone from their church to come later in the evening to meet Pastor Emmy and hear his story.

Nigel and Marian were in leadership roles within Emmanuel Church in Llandudno and both had a great heart for missions and God's world-wide family. They had met while they were both serving in the mission Operation Mobilization (OM) and after their marriage continued to serve with this organization for some years. With this background, they were eager to become involved with Pastor Emmy and understood his vision. In due course, as the link developed, they, along with Chris Spree, became the UK managers for PCM.

Interest and support grew from correspondence to visits, and since 2009 Nigel and Marian have taken teams out to Mbarara once or twice each year. Around 25% of the members of the fellowship have now had the joy of going on a team and these trips have been thrilling and life changing experiences for them. Most teams stay for two weeks and become involved in the practical and spiritual life of the ministry. Within PCM UK there are now over sixty people who sponsor children. The sponsorship enables the children to receive education; the teachers to be paid a regular wage and a food programme to ensure the children have a regular breakfast and lunch at school. PCM UK not only helps with sponsorships of children in the Kyehimba School, but also supports the work of church planting, building projects for schools, churches and the discipleship of new believers.

It soon became clear that PCM needed to become established as a charity within the UK, but rather than starting a fresh charity, Nigel and Marian's church, Emmanuel Church, kindly agreed that PCM could operate under the church's umbrella.

The 'twinning' of the two churches has been a great blessing to Emmanuel Church and helped many members in their spiritual growth and discipleship. Some of the members who went out on a team as 'baby' Christians, came back as 'teenagers', having learnt so much about dependence on the Lord and the reality of prayer.

Many learnt to pray for others and expect the Lord to answer. The children in the schools also pray for the friends in Wales and they are so blessed by that.

Sometimes the members had sicknesses or accidents while they were away and the family of God in PCM gathered around to pray for and support them.

Nigel recalls a time when he woke up in severe pain and nothing he could do brought any relief. Marian called in a couple of team members to pray, but still no relief. She then called Mellon, one of the senior adopted daughters, fervently prayed and immediately Nigel's pain disappeared. Within seconds he was fast asleep in bed, whilst the others were still in shock! Having subsequently discussed the symptoms with medics, it would appear the problem was most likely to have been kidney stones. There has been no recurrence. The following morning when Nigel woke, wondering about what had happened, he sensed the Lord saying to him, "This was to demonstrate how you need your Ugandan family more than they need you." Nigel has used this illustration in various churches in Uganda to demonstrate that the church in the West desperately needs the prayers of the Ugandan church.

Prior to Emmy and Grace's visit to Nigel and Marian's home there had been no thought of sending a team to Uganda, but the idea was born that day. Among those who attended were Chris and Jenni Spree. Next morning, as they gathered for breakfast with their two children, Sophie and Noah, they talked about Pastor Emmy and the possibility of a team from Llandudno going to visit Mbarara. Sophie, their daughter, was only eight at that time, but as she heard the discussion, her face lit up.

"Can I go?" she asked.

Chris and Jenni looked at each other with an 'Oh dear!' expression as they felt their hearts sink. Sophie was only eight, and little girls didn't go on teams to the middle of Africa! However, Chris and Jenni didn't want to deflate their daughter or flatten her spiritually, so they told her to think about it and talk to Jesus.

Nothing more was said and life continued in the normal fashion until one morning. Chris went to pull Sophie's bedroom curtains and wake her up as usual, when she suddenly said to him,

"Guess what, Daddy? I think God's told me I can go to Uganda."

Chris didn't ask Sophie how she knew that God had spoken to her, but believed her statement and spoke to his wife. Sophie was so young, but if God had spoken to her then they felt that they should somehow make it happen for her. Of course, she was far too young to go alone, so one of her parents would have to accompany her. It worked best for the family if Chris planned to go with her and Jenni stayed at home to take care of Noah and also their family cake-making business.

By the time the first team from Llandudno went to Uganda it was 2009, and Sophie was the youngest member. She was then nine years old.

The following is Sophie's testimony about that visit. She is now fifteen:

"Pastor Emmy is a wonderful man of God. I think he has such a big heart for God and the world around him.

If I had to describe Emmy in one word, it would have to be 'loving!'

He is so big and passionate for God. He loves Jesus with an unbelievably huge amount. Pastor Emmy also loves to see children safe, educated and housed. He takes care of so many orphanages and churches. There must be at least a thousand kids in his care. It doesn't bear thinking about what state that region of Uganda would be in, if it weren't for Pastor Emmy. He doesn't belittle anyone. No dream is too big. Everyone is important. No one should be overlooked.

The boy I write to from his main school wants to be a doctor when he grows up. Emmy really does encourage them to dream to do life big and aim high to achieve their heart's desires. Pastor Emmy is a brilliant role model, and I think we can all learn a lesson or two from him.

76

I went to Uganda on Emmanuel Church's first visit back in 2009 when I was nine. I remember, after believing that God had told me to go, I had great fun with fund raising and collecting toys to take out there for the kids. Pictures of me appeared in the newspaper, before and after the trip.

It was amazing to see how they all live; they own virtually nothing. The kids in the main school we visited each had a suitcase at the end of their beds, containing all their worldly possessions. They demonstrate that 'stuff' isn't what you need in order to live a good, happy life, but God is. Everyone there is so happy in all situations; they bubble over with deep joy and sing praises to God at all times.

Pastor Emmy is always very gracious and generous – constantly thinking of other's needs before his own.

I remember my Dad responding to a comment from someone at the airport on our way back. He said,

"We all left with Uganda written on our T –shirts. We are returning with it written on our hearts".

It's true. And although I haven't been back there since, it doesn't mean I shall never return; it doesn't mean that I don't remember them in my prayers; it doesn't mean I won't raise or give money to go out there and help them.

Meeting Pastor Emmy has been life-changing" (Sophie Spree, fifteen years old)

For Chris, he knows that going on this trip to Uganda had been the right thing for him to do, but he hadn't been 'bitten by the bug' in the same way as some other church members had. Nevertheless, he went back to Mbarara the following year on the second church trip in 2010, knowing that he was meant to be on that trip and had a role to play.

Although not greatly excited about returning, that trip went very well. Towards the end of the visit the rest of the team went to Queen Elizabeth Game Park for an outing. Chris had said he wouldn't go as he had been the previous year. It was just as well, because that day he became very sick with dysentery. On reflection it appears he may have caught it from his toothbrush! The previous day the team had been enacting a drama and his part had been to brush his teeth. The toothbrush had been handled rather a lot and he feels that it must have become contaminated somehow, since everyone on the team ate the same food and no one else became ill. He quickly became very sick and dehydrated due to the diarrhoea and vomiting. He was taken to the hospital, and in Uganda, you need to be accompanied by someone to care for you. Emmy stayed with him through the night and he was treated with IV infusions and medications.

"Of all the people to get sick on the team, it was best it was you" Pastor Emmy told Chris, "Because Ruth (Nigel's sister) has her daughter with her, and Nigel and Marian have their daughter, Shona, and the other team member is still a young guy".

That was true, and was in its own way a comfort to Chris. All his courses of antibiotics were finished the day before they were due to return, but they hadn't completely dealt with the problem because all the symptoms restarted on the way home. Yet, even that turned out to be a blessing. Chris and Jenny own a cake business and also Chris is a support worker for people with learning disabilities. These occupations meant that he couldn't go back to work until he was clear of all infection, so, instead, he was free to help on a stall at the RSPB summer fair. The end result was that through conversations that day he and his wife obtained a contract for supplying cakes to the R.S.P.B. (Royal Society for the Protection of Birds) in the area!

Chris has not been to Uganda since that 2010 visit. Coming home, he somehow felt in his spirit a 'completion' for him as far as trips were concerned, but he is still very involved as one of the managers of PCM UK. One of the ways he is able to help is with communication while people are away on teams and keeping others informed in order that they can pray effectively.

For Chris, one lasting impact spiritually from his visits to Uganda has been the joy of seeing his daughter hear from the Lord and being obedient even when she was so young, and his joy in being able to be a facilitator for her visit, as well his ongoing involvement in the ministry.

Chapter Nine

PCM INFLUENCE SPREADS AT HOME
AND ABROAD

Andrew, the pastor of a church in Coventry, owns a holiday chalet near Llandudno and he often visits the Christian bookshop of which Marian is a co-manager. His interest was aroused when he heard of the work in Mbarara and as a result of this, Emmy was invited to preach at his church. One of the people who attended the meeting was a young lad of fourteen years of age named Luke. This young man was struggling with a few issues at that time so he decided to stay in the main body of the church rather than attend the youth class on that particular Sunday morning; this enabled him to hear what Pastor Emmy had to say. The things he heard touched him very deeply and they made him determined to go to Uganda. Once again, as a minor, he needed to be accompanied on a mission trip to Uganda, so his mother, Dionne, went with him.

Having received a proposed programme from Pastor Emmy, Nigel requested that more visits to village churches be included in that particular trip. He suggested that the team could visit a church in the Sanga District, to which Emmy readily agreed.

On arrival at this church, as they got out of the minibus, Pastor Emmy showed them an incomplete building hidden behind the trees. It consisted of just a few poles and an iron sheet roof. It was a school! There were no floors – only trodden-down mud; no classroom furniture, just a blackboard leaning against a wall. Nonetheless, the pastor wanted it to be a PCM school! Emmy asked if PCM UK would be able to take on this new project. Nigel knew that Emmanuel Llandudno would not be able to do so, but he wondered if perhaps it would be possible for the Coventry Church to consider doing so. Even as Nigel was deliberating over this in his mind, Dionne had phoned her husband, Mark, and told him that there was a school which needed support and would they be willing to take the project on board? So that was how Kakagate School became part of PCM UK and the family in Coventry promised to raise support for it. Once again, in a remarkable way, the Lord used a young person to forge the link with the ministry in Uganda.

Emmanuel Church, Llandudno, is responsible for the school at Kyehimba. This was an existing school that had been started by the local church, but which was struggling to keep going. The Ugandan government had wanted to take the school over and make it a secular school, but the church had refused to allow this to happen. Then the schools' inspector arrived and confiscated all the textbooks – leaving the teachers with nothing! One of the PCM staff, Emmy D, the driver, came from this area and he petitioned Pastor Emmy to take the school over. This happened several times and although Pastor Emmy had said that it just wasn't possible, the church went ahead and put up a sign anyway, declaring it to be a PCM School! So Pastor Emmy promised to take a team to visit them and see how the team responded, whether the Lord would put it on their hearts to support the school.

The team from Wales were taken there on their next visit. The children had memorised long speeches and there were local dignitaries present, all beseeching PCM UK to take on their support.

The response of the team was to promise to pray about the situation. They knew it would take time to raise the money to improve the school and build it up and they prayed for thirty sponsors to come forward over the next two years.

The Lord began to provide an answer to these prayers. One non-Christian donor provided £1,000 for desks. Gradually the buildings were improved, with concrete floors being poured, then new classrooms added. In 2014 the Primary 7 final examinations revealed that Kyehimba School was the top school in the district in spite of the fact that this was the very first year the school had a Primary Seven class.

About 10% of the students are orphans. The guardians / parents and community all contribute as much as they are able to in order to help with school expenses. Although many of the children now have sponsors in Wales, their carers still contribute as well, so that all students are treated in the same way. Now the children proudly wear the PCM schools' uniform, and are not only receiving a good education, but are also well fed each day. It has become a two-way blessing, for not only does the church in Llandudno have a burden for Kyehimba School, but the schoolchildren also have a burden for the church and their sponsors, and pray for them.

The coordinator at the school is Fraim. He has always been a leading force behind the improvement and continuation of the school. Fraim's family have lived in the village of Kyhimba for seventeen years. His father was the first Christian in the area. This is the story of how he became a Christian. He suffered a very long illness and in spite of spending a lot of money in consultations with the witch doctors, he got no better. Then a friend suggested that he make a long trip north to Bushenyi as he had heard that missionaries lived there who might be able to help him. Fraim's father made the trip and the missionaries were only too glad to pray with him. The Lord healed him and he was convinced that he must change his life and serve the Lord from that time forward. It was he who, having returned to the area around Kyehimba, began to tell others about Jesus. Twenty seven years ago a small church was started, led by him. This small church had the first vision to start a school in Kyehimba, not just to educate children, but also to teach them about the love of God shown to us in Jesus. There were many orphaned and needy children in the area. The school began with thirty-six pupils, twenty boys and sixteen girls. It was because so many of the children lacked parental care and love that Fraim petitioned Pastor Emmy to allow them to join the group. Fraim is completely committed to continuing his father's vision.

The sponsorship scheme has made such a difference to the school, not just in education, but in feeding the children, buying further land for expansion, paying salaries for workers and teachers, constructing classrooms, dormitories and buying beds – the list is endless! There are future hopes and dreams, too, to purchase more land; build a school hall; and then buy a vehicle to transport children from Kyehimba to the PCM Secondary School in Katyazo.

Chapter Ten

TRACEY'S STORY

Visits to Uganda have been life changing for many of the Emmanuel, Llandudno members. No one has been excluded from going on a trip because of their youth or older age, or the length they have been a Christian. Tracey had only been a Christian for three months when she went on her first team trip. She had met Pastor Emmy and heard the story of his life and work and decided she would go along because two other ladies from the church, with whom she was friendly, had committed to go on the team trip.

"After all," she said to me, "You've got to do something when you are forty!" So Tracey went along to the meeting for people interested on going on the team to Uganda. During the meeting she felt a confirmation in her spirit that she should go when the name of one of the children flashed up on the screen and it was the name of someone she knew well. Somehow that simple coincidence clinched the matter for her. However, there were obstacles to overcome.

Tracey is a single mum, and the trip coincided with her son's twentieth birthday. Could she not be around for his special day? Then, there was the question of money. Again, as a single mother, could she afford this trip? Africa? Could she really do a trip to Africa? Then, what about the commitment – could she manage that?

Was she just being swayed by the momentum and emotion of it all? It all seemed well 'out of her league!'

However, things went ahead and she began to prepare. Not long before she went, she began to feel guilty about going. She didn't understand much about the Christian faith, let alone how to share it – and she felt guilty about the money which she was spending. She had never spent such a large sum at once! Another issue was to pay for the required immunisations and anti-malarial drugs (they are very costly) and she was also required to raise funds for the work of PCM.

It was even difficult answering the questions asked by her work colleagues and friends because Tracey actually knew very little about where she was going or what she would be doing. She had met Pastor Emmy and seen his presentation, but apart from that she knew very little.

Even the travelling was a new experience for Tracey. The team consisted of eight people, three of whom were women about her age. Somehow, wearing the PCM T-shirt and being herded around the airport made her feel like a child on a school trip. When she finally sank into her seat on the plane she laughed at it all! What was she doing, flying to a foreign country with people she hardly knew? She was used to living on her own and now she would be living with a group and she wondered how well she would cope.

Tracey's memories of that first trip are still vivid. Her first impressions are of arriving at Entebbe Airport and taking photos of the birds. Then Pastor Emmy and his driver, Emmy D, arrived and they began the five-hour-long journey west to Mbarara. Tracey remembers her surprise and delight at seeing a monkey on the road at Masaka, the town halfway between Kampala and Mbarara. Also she was amazed when they stopped there and had a Coke to drink! As they drove along, many people waved to them and she noticed the large advertisements along the roadside with interest. Finally the team arrived in Mbarara and were housed in two rented houses next-door to each other in the Moslem area of the town. Each of the houses had large iron gates. 'Are these to keep the lions out?' she wondered to herself.

Every morning the team were awakened by the 5.30 am call to prayer sounded out by the mosque. Until she became used to the sound of it, she woke up in terror. Then the old bus arrived to take them to the school orphanage and they drove through the busy rush-hour traffic where everyone was honking horns. It was so different from Llandudno!

Arriving at the PCM Mbarara School was a revelation. The gates opened and the children started singing. As the team got out of the bus, the children danced round them, trying to hold their hands. There was such joy! It was truly overwhelming! Then the children started to pray – just as they were, in their bare feet, standing in the dust, and Tracey found it so moving.

Life began to fall into a slightly haphazard routine for the team. They were very challenged by the lack of water and electricity. It was hard to understand the children's speech, and the children found it hard to understand the team. One child was overheard to say that the Mzungu (white people) spoke another language – the goats' language!

The day-to-day living in Uganda changed the way that Tracey looked at life. It put a lot of things into a true perspective, and spiritually she began to understand that there was a difference between living with God and living for God. She learnt to adjust to having people all around her, living with her and loving her. It impressed her so much to see the children totally reliant upon God for everything. They lived very hard lives and were utterly grateful even when they were given the smallest gift, and always seemed full of joy. Their little faces were always beaming!

Tracey had gone on the team thinking it would be a 'once in a lifetime' adventure, but it didn't prove to be that. She has felt compelled to go again and again. Even so, it was not without personal cost or fear. She has learnt to trust the Lord to provide for and take care of her. Once she felt very unsafe when she was going to an evangelistic crusade meeting because she had been told about an evangelist at a similar meeting who had acid thrown in his face by an ex-Imam because the gospel was being preached.

Some deep impressions still remain. On her first visit to Kyehimba to see the school which is supported by PCM UK and her church, Tracey was haunted by the vacant eyes of the children – now these children are really happy and cared for.

Once she went to the funeral of the grandmother of Mellon, one of the older children who has been part of the Parental Care family for a long time. It was not a Christian funeral, but held according to traditional customs. Tracey found it very oppressive and the children who attended were so scared of the 'mzungu' people. They looked at their white faces and thought they must be dead, too.

Other traumatic memories were some of the stories which she heard in the women's prison in Mbarara. Some women were in prison just because they tried to stand up for themselves as women! Many had come to know and love the Lord and they prayed for the visiting team. Such times are always so humbling.

On her first visit, in the main church, the team were introduced, one by one. The congregation was told that there were three 'babies' – new Christians, and Tracey was the newest arrival! Then the people surged forward, asking the Mzungu visitors to pray for them. Tracey found herself in a situation where she had to totally rely on the Lord to help her as she prayed for those dear people. She had never experienced anything like this before, and it was scary!

Tracey comments, "In the West we are isolated, impoverished spiritually and socially." We have so much to learn from our African brothers and sisters and how we can be prayer partners for each other.

In 2013 Tracey knew that she would not be able to go on the church team because part of her work as a psychology lecturer in Bangor University involves the preparation for the graduation ceremonies and in 2013 graduation day was set at the time the team were to be in Uganda. Yet Tracey's friend, Jo, had a dream that she was on the team. She didn't know what to make of that, for it was an impossibility!

Tracey was learning that nothing is impossible with God! Not only were the dates of the graduation changed, (something quite unheard of!) but also the money for the trip was wonderfully provided! That visit proved another blessing in many ways as she learnt to trust in the Lord to give her a message to say at a church service, when there had been little time to prepare beforehand. She was learning about the faithfulness of God, who never calls us to mission without providing and equipping.

Of course coming home becomes a challenge, too! There is a reverse culture shock coming home and reconnecting with family, work and the frenetic society in which we live!

Chapter Eleven

IMPACTED LIVES

Almost everyone who comes in contact with Pastor Emmy finds that their lives are changed by the encounter. One such person is Peter Frith, and subsequent to his encounter with the pastor, he also had become involved in PCM UK.

It all began when Emmy and Sarah were able to move into their concrete bungalow in Mbarara. Emmy had always wanted to entertain a team from UK, but before he had the house, it was almost impossible. He used to have to find hotel rooms for his guests. This was a costly undertaking and not many young people were able to afford that sort of accommodation when coming to serve on a team. It also isolated the team from the ordinary people who they had come to serve. Once he had a house of his own, he was in a position to invite a team from Signpost International to come and visit.

Peter's eldest daughter, Helen, had been working with Signpost in the Philippines for a gap year and her experience had been very good, so when they advertised in 2005 for candidates for a short-term mission trip to Uganda, he had no hesitation in allowing his younger daughter, Rachel, to apply. Part of that trip was spent in Mbarara, working with Pastor Emmy. Rachel's lasting impression is that of feeling humbled and mortified as Emmy and his family gave up their beds for the visiting team to use.

Following Rachel's visit, Pastor Emmy and his eldest daughter, Grace, came to UK and were able to visit the Frith family in Mansfield, so the bond between the two families was forged. Since that visit Peter has met with Pastor Emmy on several of his subsequent visits to UK and has been very impressed to learn how God is using Emmy and his family. Many times Emmy has asked Peter to visit Mbarara and see the work for himself, but until 2014 logistically it proved too difficult for him to do so. It was a great thrill when he was able to join the PCM team led by Nigel and Marian that October! It changed Peter's understanding of the situation to see the ministry in action, 'on the ground.' Everything he had previously learnt about the ministry now became reality! There remains a lasting memory of how warmly they were received wherever they went. On that trip Peter began to see the enormity of all that Emmy and Sarah have achieved in bringing the Kingdom of God here on earth. Visiting the many schools and churches that PCM supports was a very humbling experience. Peter says, "It has been both a privilege and a pleasure to have had a small part in this, I have always been impressed by Emmy's humility. I also know he is a man of prayer. Time and time again he sends me emails for my prayer requests. In many ways he supports me more than I support him!"

What a great testimony and one that many others who have met Emmy can echo.

Chapter Twelve
LIFE AS A PREACHER'S KID

I asked Grace, the eldest of Pastor Emmy's biological children, what it had been like to grow up as a child in a family which keeps on expanding. Grace is now a mature young lady of twenty-five years of age. She is married to Tomson Nowamani and they have a delightful two-year-old boy called Tomi Teshi (meaning rich, bright and strong). Tomi is now the second generation as a 'preacher's kid,' as Tomson is in ministry at the Pentecostal Life Church in Kampala.

Grace's experiences as a preacher's kid have left her with a burden for other children and young people whose parents are in full-time ministry and she and her husband have now started their own ministry, 'Preacher's Kids Restoration Ministries.'

~

As Grace looks back over her childhood, she remembers how hard her life was in the early days. She was still very small when the Lord called her parents to minister far away from their home village to a new place where they were strangers. The family had no guaranteed income and they lived by faith. Grace used to go with her mum, Sarah, to work in other people's shambas (garden plots) in order to get even a little food for the family to eat. It is almost unthinkable now that a pastor's wife should have to go out and dig for other people in order to get a little food for her own table. Sarah worked so hard all day and all through the season until the crops were harvested. Most of the food was for the owner of the shamba and just a little was given to Sarah for her family. Even though it was very hard, the Lord did provide for them all. Normally there was just one small meal each day, and that, Grace commented, wasn't a very nice one either!

Life was hard. Grace recalls how her mum made her a black, dotted dress by hand, out of her own old skirt. It was all Grace had, so it had to be washed each night, ready to be worn the next day. There were no beds, so Grace had a sack filled with dry grass for her mattress and slept on the floor with just a sheet. At times food was so scarce that they could only have a drink consisting of a few tea leaves soaked in hot water and drunk without sugar or milk instead of their evening meal. No wonder Grace confesses to feeling envious of children who had better lives! Sometimes there was no paraffin to light the lamp in the house, so the meal, such as it was, had to be served outside in order for them to see a little from the electric lights in their neighbour's house. The neighbours were often so unkind that when they saw the family about to eat they would turn off their lights and leave them to eat in darkness!

Footwear was also a problem. Sometimes they had none and on other occasions had to get anything they could, regardless of shape or size or even if they matched – in order to have something on their feet. Grace tried hard to feel grateful and to pretend she looked smart. At school there was always the worry of being sent back home and not allowed to attend because the fees had not been paid. Sometimes Grace would hide near the school in the bushes when the head teacher had sent her away and once the head had left the classroom, she would sneak back in! In Uganda, as in most of Africa, the pupils are so eager to learn and get a good education, for without that they are unable to get a good job and break the vicious circle of poverty.

Grace also had another problem to contend with, and this continued throughout her schooling. She often had severe back pain, even resulting at times in temporary paralysis of her legs. Grace struggled with all these things and didn't know how to cope with the problems, finding it very difficult to share how she felt, even to her parents or friends. However, looking back, she can see how God was in the situation, watching over the family and protecting them.

Grace's parents continued to faithfully serve the Lord in spite of the difficulties they faced on a daily basis. Their family had grown to include two girls, Grace and Faith, followed by two boys, Daniel and Roger, soon to be followed by Marie Julie, along with the adopted family, Falida, Ayisha, Imam, and Mariam The eight children all loved each other and got on well. Even though there was so little, Grace does not remember any of the 'birth' children feeling resentful about their 'spiritual' sisters.

In 2003, by the grace of God, enough money had been raised to buy a really good house for the family and this was a turning point for them all. They moved into a three-bedroom house with a garage, kitchen and indoor bathroom and toilets. For the children it seemed like living in a dream and Grace took her whole school class to the house to see the miracle home and felt so proud to live in such a lovely place! The home was so large that the family could expand further and more needy children were added. There was great happiness as the family shared the home together. For Grace, her joy became even greater, as when she had passed primary 7, she was enabled through sponsor grandmother (Jaaja) to go to a boarding school in Kampala. In Uganda it is normal for all secondary schools to be boarding schools. It is thought that it gives the children a better opportunity to study well without the worries of doing chores at home.

Although there were times when Grace was very homesick for her close and loving family and she often wept for them, she was thrilled to study at the secondary school. Sadly, she was only able to complete one year there because the back pain and leg paralysis continued to cause problems.

Although Grace was seen by paediatricians and neurologists, no clear diagnosis was made. Because of this, the decision was made for her to continue at a secondary school in Mbarara, in order to be closer to home. Grace's progress through secondary school was spasmodic, due to her continuing health problems, but she was a good student and tried to learn as much as possible through the years. Her thirst for knowledge led Grace to eventually return to Kampala to study on an I.T. course in 2009. It proved once again to be a difficult time for her. She was still not well, but worked hard and attended a good church where she met a young pastor who began to court her. Grace fell in love with him and believed he loved her. The young man had met her parents and relatives and the introduction wedding was being organised. (In Uganda an introduction wedding is a very big ceremony where the bride price is agreed upon and the families give their young people to each other). This is followed by a civil service and a church wedding. However, Grace began to hear rumours about her fiancée, that he had another girlfriend and was cheating on her. He might have loved Grace for the sweet, godly young lady she was, but this other woman was well off and supplied all his needs, so he loved her for her money and material goods! Grace wisely broke the engagement, but it was at great emotional cost, for she was heartbroken and lost her self-esteem. Yet, she was also grateful that the Lord had allowed her to see the man as he really was before they made their vows and finalized the marriage.

Grace returned home for a time of healing. Surrounded by her loving family and their prayers, she was able to help in the ministry by using her skills to help get sponsors for the many children in the Parental Care School. She used her IT skills to make promotional videos of the children which were used in UK and USA. Grace is also gifted as a songwriter and wrote songs for them to sing. Now there is a PCM children's choir which travels in USA sharing God's love and blessing people there.

When Grace felt healed and ready to face the wider world once again, she applied to do a social work and administration course, once again in the capital, Kampala. While studying there, she caught the eye of a fellow student, and the attraction was mutual. His name was Tomson Nowamani. He is now her beloved husband. They became engaged while at college and decided to marry and finish their course as a married couple.

All of Grace's experiences have taught her to rely on God and prove His faithfulness through all the trials and problems which life holds. The Nnyanzi family have surrounded her with love and prayers and rejoiced to see her grow in her faith and develop into a woman of God. Grace's latest venture is to set up a small business in order to raise funds to help other preachers' kids within the ministry she and Tomson have started.

All of the Nnyanzi biological children can echo her feelings that it was a privilege to grow up in such a home, even though they had to face so many challenges, especially in the early days.

Chapter Thirteen
THE STORY OF AN 'ADOPTED' DAUGHTER

When I visited the Nnyanzi family in 2002, long before Parental Care Ministries was set up, a young lady called Beatrice, was already part of their adopted family. It wasn't that she was an orphan and had no parents; in fact, she is the daughter of Rose and Martin, in whose house the church was planted when Emmy and Sarah moved to Mbarara from Ishongororo. Beatrice is the eldest of their children and was saved when her mother took her to the crusade meeting near the police station in Ishongororo. At that time she was six or seven years of age. Although her father had work as a policeman, the pay was not sufficient for him to educate his family. Beatrice was sent to school when she turned three, but as there was no money to pay the school fees, she was constantly sent back home and told to get the needed fees. This pattern continued for seven years, and Beatrice missed so much of her education that she was never able to finish Primary Seven or graduate to secondary school.

Her father was never antagonistic to the gospel, and was more than willing for Pastor Emmy to begin the church in his Mbarara home. However, he has always felt that as his work requires him to carry a gun, this prohibited him from taking the step of salvation. (This untrue belief persisted for years, and now in 2015 he has three years left before retirement and promises to become a Christian when he no longer will be carrying a gun.)

Beatrice's lack of education has always been a deep grief to her. Instead of attending school, from the age of six she was more often to be found digging in the fields. Seeing other children on their way to and from school made her miserable; she couldn't bear to look at them because it was just too painful to do so. This was her way of life until she was fourteen, when she made a momentous decision that she would not waste her life, but use it, with or without education, to minister to others about the Lord.

At this time her father received a posting to Ibanda, so the family moved away, but Beatrice stayed with Emmy and Sarah. They taught her so much, encouraging her to stand firm in the faith and trust the Lord, however difficult the circumstances. She grew as a big sister to the Nnyanzi children, helping in the family with the daily chores. By this time, Sarah had given birth to her fifth child, a daughter, Marie Julie, and Beatrice helped to look after her. During this time, Emmy and Sarah provided the means for her to attend adult education classes and learn to read, write and speak good English. Always a bright girl, she learnt very well.

As Beatrice grew up, her thoughts turned to marriage. However, there seemed to be no one in their church whom she could marry, and with whom she could start a Christian family. Her longing and prayer was to marry a Christian young man, so that they could serve the Lord together. She had seen that ideal working out in practice in the lives of her 'foster' parents, Sarah and Emmy.

In due course, her prayer was answered when Evard joined their church. He loved the Lord and became involved in the choir, going out with the team on crusades and local evangelism. For two years they ministered side by side in these outreach efforts and as worship leaders in the church, they prayed for each other and both of them prayed for a spouse. They fell in love with each other and found that their prayers for a spouse were answered!

Although Evard didn't have enough money to pay the dowry price, and is still saving to buy the last two cows required, they were given permission to marry in 2007. Life was not easy for the new couple as Evard tried to make a living and support Beatrice and also continue in ministry. There is so much unemployment in Uganda and those who manage to find work are often paid a pittance. However, gradually the couple became established and started their longed-for family.

Not only has it been their desire to raise a family who would be taught the things of God and learn to love Him, but also Beatrice has always had a burden for other girls who are struggling to get an education, as she did.

She knows that without the loving care of Emmy and Sarah and being able to live with them in their home and receive some education, she probably would have ended up on the streets. Girls, such as she was, are very vulnerable in Uganda. Even to get very lowly work in a hotel as a maid, a girl needs to have been educated up to at least Senior 4. For a girl without any education, the only prospects are to work in the gardens or to be a servant. Without an education, either a father or a husband needs to support such a girl until she marries.

Over the past eight years ten girls have come to live with Beatrice and Evard, all of whom were in similar situations as that which she had experienced. In fact, one of the girls is her own biological sister. It is a struggle to care for them all, but the couple love them and try to get school fees for them in order that they can finish their education and eventually get work and be able to support themselves. Beatrice and Evard now have four children of their own and a fifth is expected. Evard has a steady job as a taxi driver and he owns his own vehicle, which is a great blessing, as is the fact that they now have their own house – even if it is rather crowded! It is a happy home, filled with love and laughter. Beatrice acknowledges that finding a good husband has brought her healing from the inward pain she felt as a child. She is still very involved in ministry as a worship leader, sometimes preaching, helping with teaching seminars and fellowship home groups. She has grown to be an inspiration to the youth of the church.

Reflecting over the years she spent with Emmy and Sarah, Beatrice comments:

> "Life with Supermom (Sarah's nickname) and Dad and so many children was good, but most of the time, very hard. Children came and went as they couldn't live with just depending on God. There was sometimes only posho (maize porridge) and beans for a whole week."

However, Beatrice persevered, even when there was no food. She prayed to be kept strong in the Lord. Several girls did leave the family, married quickly and are still suffering from their poor choices. Sarah always encouraged Beatrice through the bad times, "God will provide; be strong!"

Through the years with Emmy and Sarah, Beatrice recalls some of the lessons she has learnt:

1. To love children

2. To serve God

3. What a godly marriage is like

4. It is good to be hospitable, welcoming visitors

5. It is good to persevere through tough situations.

All these lessons have been put into practice in her own married life, for life has been tough for Beatrice and Evard. Her biggest dream is to grow more and more into the ministry she shares with her husband, to raise her children well and do whatever God asks of her. Her prayer and joy is to give to others what they would not be able to get on their own – parental care and love! As well as the girls who live with them in order to receive an education, many local children also find a welcome in their home. So the work started by Emmy and Sarah continues to grow and expand in the lives of those they have helped, as they also reach out to children in need.

Chapter Fourteen

PERSONAL REFLECTIONS

As I look back over my own long life, there have been several occasions when I have met people, or they have walked over the threshold into my life, and I have been instantly aware of the presence of the Lord in them. The impact on my own life has been immediate and long lasting.

There was a time when as mother to three young children and with a husband who, having been diagnosed with an incurable neurological disease and struggling with depression, I was finding it hard to be strong in the Lord. Financially, things were very tight, as our work was in full-time Christian service. Sometimes it was quite hard to find the money to feed the family adequately, let alone buy school uniforms or sports equipment. However, one principle my husband I adhered to and always tried to put into practice, right from the start of our married life was, 'be given to hospitality.' Missionaries travelling back to USA from Africa often stayed with us, as well as many other friends who needed 'a bed' in London for one reason or the other. So many times we were blessed and encouraged by these visits, but there were three people who impacted me greatly. From the moment they came through the front door, they radiated the love and joy of Jesus. Just being with them revived my spirit – one of them was a young, single girl who had been 'disappointed in love,' yet had never allowed that to embitter her; another was a young pastor who my husband had known as a child. Sadly, his life ended when he was only forty-nine, due to a road accident, and the third was the pastor who discipled me as a young Christian. How I thank God for all of them, for they showed me such glimpses of Jesus, that I was left with a longing to press on in my spiritual life and find a deeper joy and be able to radiate His love to others, too.

When I first met Emmy and Sarah, I recognised this same deep joy in the Lord and felt His love being radiated to me. Instantly I was drawn to them and was more than happy to keep in contact with them after our first meeting. Their deep, but humble spirituality made it easy for me to respond to their invitation to visit them in Mbarara, and share in the work of preaching the gospel in the villages around. From this visit I heard the Lord asking me to be willing to help them and a great longing grew within me to see them living in better circumstances. As I explained in the introduction to this book, I was broken inside when I saw the house which they were renting and where they normally lived.

Towards the end of my visit, Emmy, Sarah and I talked together about their housing needs and the need for a church building. For my visit they had rented a small house in Mbarara, opposite that was a large house which was for sale. From curiosity mixed with the stirrings of faith, I suggested we visit the estate agent and enquire about the building and the price. It was a lot of money! We chatted with the agent about housing in the area and it helped me to understand the sort of sum which would be required to purchase a brick house, large enough for their family. Even though the cost was very reasonable compared with UK prices, it seemed a huge amount of money, way beyond what I might even dream of raising. After all, what could one widow who had retired from work and had so little money that she needed to sell her home and find a smaller one in order to release some capital, do to help? Common sense told me that I could do no more than pray into this dream of a house for my lovely friends in Uganda, but the Holy Spirit kept tugging at my heartstrings and reminding me that I had promised to 'lay up treasure in heaven,' knowing God had promised to meet all my needs. Once I had arrived back home, God began to move in a mighty way and money poured into the 'House for Emmy and Sarah' fund. Trusting the Lord to provide for the house was one of the most exciting adventures on which God has taken me. I have seen the Lord provide in amazing ways both before and since that time, but it was such a great adventure because it was the start of something much greater which God wanted to do. Never in my wildest dreams could I have envisioned that by 2015 there would be six primary schools and one secondary school, caring for over 2,000 vulnerable children in the Ankole district! To me, it was just a case of giving my 'widow's mite' to God so that Sarah and Emmy and their growing family could be well housed and not have to spend money on rent – but the Lord had planned something so much greater.

One day Sarah and I went for a walk, just looking around in Mbarara area. She opened her heart to me and told me how much she would love a farm – to have a big 'shamba' and cows. She also dared to dream her dream and tell the Lord about it. The last time when I was able to visit these dear friends in Uganda she took me to see the new land at Katyazo, purchased by PCM where the secondary school would be built, and later another primary school. She showed me the banana plantation: the cows, the chickens, and the muddy hole which would be the fish farm! Her dream was becoming reality! How greatly the Lord has blessed and how much has been accomplished in a relatively short time.

It has been a huge lesson to me and also a great encouragement – to be faithful in the small things which the Lord asks me to do, and then to watch and see how He multiplies beyond our wildest dreams! How does the Lord do this? It is by His Holy Spirit touching other hearts, giving them a vision, making them willing to do what He asks – and this is how the work of PCM has expanded. Each person is one small link, joining together to make a strong chain – a chain of love which is keeping vulnerable children safe and teaching them to know the Lord. So many people, young and old alike, have been faithful in small things, and together they have enabled God's kingdom to grow in Uganda. So, if God has put a dream into your heart, then pray into it and trust Him to fulfil it, even though it might seem an impossibility. With God, we are told, 'all things are possible!'"

Emmy and Sarah's great love for the Lord has warmed many hearts, so that others have come alongside to help. Now, as well as in Uganda, there is also PCM in UK and USA.

Chapter Fifteen
HELP COMES FROM THE USA

One amazing fact about the story of PCM is the way in which the Lord has used children to speak into the lives of adults and bring them alongside to help with the work. The Holy Spirit used the words which a little girl in America had written in a Christmas card to her mother, to bring about the connection between Mbarara and Texas which He wanted to forge!

It all began when Monica Barret, the wife of a successful paediatrician went to collect her daughter Libby from school in December 2006. Libby was in the third grade (8-9 year olds), and the class had a project to make Christmas cards. Libby proudly brought her beautifully gift-wrapped card and handed it as a present to her mother. It was only addressed to her, not to both parents. This card would dramatically change the life of her mother and eventually of the entire family.

When Monica opened the card she read this:

"Glory to God in the Highest and Peace on
Earth to men."
May the Christmas song the angels sang stir
In our hearts again.

Dear Mom, I feel this Christmas, we should

Be missionaries and help the poor.
Jesus keeps pushing me to tell you. Merry
Christmas.
Love, Libby.

After reading the card, as soon as she was back home, Monica dropped to her knees on the kitchen floor and prayed, "OK, God, you've got my attention. What do you want me to do?"

She waited quietly and then she remembered reading a book about an orphanage in Mozambique and at once a name of someone she knew who was involved in this project, sprang into her mind. She felt the Lord telling her to phone this person, which she did, only to learn that a trip was being planned to take a team to visit the orphanage, in the following month of January 2007.

Very soon after receiving this card Monica had a strange dream. She saw a toddler sitting in a box. His legs were hanging outside of the box and it was pouring with rain, and it was also night time. A single street lamp was behind the child and he sat absolutely still – it was as if he was just trying to survive.

This dream stayed with Monica and she realized that God was trying to capture her attention both through the card and now the dream.

Monica's phone call resulted in her being invited to join the team going to Mozambique – and although she now felt sure this was the way the Lord was leading her, she also was terrified of travelling to Africa, leaving her husband and girls behind. Mark, Monica's husband, was equally horrified. His wife didn't like travelling to Dallas, just ninety miles away – how would she cope with going half way around the world! The winter months were also his busiest time at work, so who would look after him and Bailey, who was eleven years old, and Libby who was even younger? Then there were the potential dangers from tropical illnesses and insurgent fighters. Mark was not a happy man, and he was definitely against the plan.

Monica knew the Lord wanted her on the team to Mozambique and time for inoculations and buying airline tickets was getting short; but she wouldn't go against her husband's wishes. She just prayed and asked the Lord to deal with the situation. Of course, He did! He sent a friend to make an unexpected visit to Mark, a well-trusted older pastor with whom he could share and receive counsel. Soon after this, Mark picked up a magazine and glancing through it, found an article concerning a woman who had gone to Mozambique on her own – and he knew the Lord was speaking to him, convincing him that Monica should join the team and that she would be in His safe keeping. So Monica went. It was a huge step. For some time, as Mark's medical practice had blossomed and they had climbed the social ladder, so their spiritual lives had become stagnant, but this trip threw her back on the Lord in a mighty way.

Monica's expectations on the trip were far from fulfilled. She found herself living in a small hut with three other ladies. What was wrong? She felt so out of place and struggling to be aware of God's presence with her.

"What in the world am I doing here in Africa?" she prayed, feeling let down and disappointed by the whole experience.

God was soon to show her.

While she was there, another visitor came to the place where she was staying. There were meetings taking place and Pastor Emmy had felt compelled to go from Uganda and support his friend Leon, who was preaching in Mozambique, even though he didn't have the money for the flight. When Emmy ministered at one of the meetings and gave his testimony, Monica knew she had to speak to him. Her heart had been touched so deeply by his story. Her own pain from her damaged childhood surfaced as she listened to him talk about his childhood. As soon as she met Pastor Emmy, a strong spiritual connection was forged. Now she knew why she had needed to make the trip to Mozambique – it was to meet Emmy! Now Emmy knew why he had to make that trip to Mozambique – it was to meet Monica!

Emmy's recollection of that meeting was,

"When I met Dr Barret's wife and we talked and prayed, I knew she was the reason why I had come. Out of all the people there, I knew we had met for God's divine purposes."

After Monica had returned to her home in Tyler, Texas, the family kept in touch with Emmy by email. Her husband, Mark, often emailed late at night and felt he had made a 'best friend' on the other side of the world, even though they had never met. The more they learnt about Emmy, Sarah and the PCM schools, the more Mark and Monica longed to go and see the work for themselves, so in March 2008 instead of a planned skiing holiday, the whole family went to Uganda. Their friends were not at all supportive of this adventure and there seemed to be many obstacles thrown in their way, yet, in spite of it all, they finally made their first mission trip.

The reality of what they found came as a real shock. By this time there were 120 children in the Parental Care School. It was a primary boarding school, but all the buildings were primitive structures. The children slept on the floors on thin foam mattresses. Eight teachers gave their services for the love of Jesus, for no money was available for salaries. The water supply was from the river which ran near the school. It was dirty, muddy water which had to be collected in jerry cans. This in itself was a great danger, and tragically, Emmy's nephew had been drowned while he was fetching water from the river.

The food which the children ate was very meagre, and each day they prayed in faith for provision. The records show that in 900 days, there were only two days when there was no provision of food at all, even though on other days one or two meals might be missing. The meals were mostly porridge made from maize flour (posho) and beans. The majority of the children were clad in old, ragged clothes and had no shoes on their feet. Even so, the children abounded with joy and thanked God for all He had provided for them!

Mark and Monica knew they needed to help; how would they manage to raise funds, as Mark had a busy medical practice to manage? Mark thought maybe they could find a professional fund raiser to work on their behalf, but Emmy knew that the Lord wanted Mark to be the PCM representative in the USA and that little by little the Lord would lead and help them.

In spite of many early difficulties, the Lord did open the way and within six weeks of sending application papers, the U.S. government granted them the charity status they needed. Gradually sponsors were found for some of the children, and money was given for beds, a clean water supply, uniforms, textbooks, desks and salaries for the staff. After a while other people began to visit on short-term mission teams to help with the work and in the fullness of time, Emmy was granted a visa for a twenty-day visit to Texas. By the time this happened there was an enthusiastic board of directors in the USA and a growing number of sponsors and supporters. The God who delights in making the impossible possible was once again working miracles! One single donor gave the money needed for a sixty-eight acre plot at Katyazo, where the building of a PCM headquarters compound was begun. There is now a secondary school, a farm, dormitories, library, church and a multi-purpose meeting room. A baby home for under-school-age children has just started, the building of a new primary school has begun, and plans are in hand for guest houses, and a clinic for use of the local people. There will be playing fields, football pitches and netball courts. The site is outside the city, near the small airstrip. It is a lovely country setting for the children to grow up in.

What an amazing God we have! All this has sprung from a Christmas card written by a young child, with a message in it prompted by Jesus! When we are willing to be obedient to the Lord, even though we may feel totally inadequate for the task, totally out of our 'comfort zone,' God is able to do far more than we can ask or think!

Chapter Sixteen

NO MAN IS AN ISLAND

How often have these words written by the poet John Donne, been quoted! We were created to live in community, not as isolated human beings. When we encounter other people, our lives are impacted forever. They should be enriched through meeting another person, although sadly this is not always the case. However, everyone whom I know who has met Emmy has been impacted by his friendliness, joy and love of the Lord.

This testimony has been sent to me from Janice Nind, a lady who met Pastor Emmy and Sarah for the first time in 2001 when we were both on a mission trip to Rwanda:

"I first met Emmy in Rwanda. What a commitment of love it was that the Nnyanzi's travelled so far to see their friend Hugh Henderson, especially since Sarah was heavily pregnant with her fifth child and experiencing difficulty in walking.

Emmy always smiled; even after hearing my testimony he and Sarah could just see the Lord at work in everything I had told them. (This dear lady had suffered because of a very difficult childhood, made some extremely bad choices in her early adult life, which resulted in abusive relationships, drug addiction and a prison term. She also managed to survive terminal ovarian cancer and still bring up her two children as a single mother.)

A few years after Janice's initial meeting with Emmy, she was able to travel on the first Signpost International mission team to Mbarara, to help at Pastor Emmy's church. This is her comment about that trip:

"Our first trip to Mbarara was a real lesson in loving and sharing all that God has given us. The children gave up their beds and bedrooms to us; all the family and relations ate outside while we were inside, sitting at the table and eating food, which they had especially prepared for us. They went out of their way to try to cook food which they knew we would enjoy. Then the family and friends would come in and enjoy praising the Lord with us. It was such a gift from God to be there with these special people."

Although this was a few years before the establishment of Parental Care Ministries, there were many children already living with them in the family.

"Emmy has a very special love for children, not just his own biological family, but for all children. He and Sarah have spent their lives helping to make education possible for all children, regardless of whether or not anyone can provide school fees for them or even feed them at home. All the children are taught and fed regardless of their backgrounds. Emmy and Sarah have worked tirelessly in fundraising and procuring sponsors at home and abroad to help the children.

In order to achieve this, Emmy and Sarah, (who is nicknamed Supermom) have been willing to travel to Europe and America to tell others about the children and their needs. Pastor Emmy has encouraged Christians all over the world to care about children and informed them of ways in which they can help to bring the love of Jesus into the children's lives."

Janice's final comment is: "He (Emmy) will never give up on God. What a privilege to have worked with this man."

Many of us can say 'amen' to that statement!

It has not been easy for Pastor Emmy and Sarah to make the long journey from Uganda to UK or America. Often these trips have been made during the winter months, and they have endured snow and ice and bitter winds – so different from the warm equatorial climate of Western Uganda! They have graciously eaten the unfamiliar food which has been put before them, always blessing their hosts with their love and with their prayers. Sometimes while they have been travelling they have had phone calls telling them of problems back at Mbarara, yet they have still continued to speak at meetings and fulfil engagements in spite of heavy hearts.

The final part of this story is given to Pastor Emmy – for him to share his own reflections of the journey on which the Lord has taken him over the past fifteen years. Emmy recalls that when the Lord gave him the name, Parental Care Ministries, he accepted it as a title for the work, but at that time he didn't really appreciate the full meaning of the words. However, the experience of these past fifteen years has shown him that there are thousands of people all over the world who have lacked parental love and care. So many people have broken hearts and are full of pain because they have lacked this special love which their parents should have given them. It isn't just children who are in need, but many adults still suffer because they have not experienced the love and care they deserved in their childhood. Indeed such parental love and care should be the birthright of every child.

Emmy wants to remind readers of the words of King David said in Psalm 27:10, (NIV): "Though my father and mother forsake me, the Lord will receive me."

He testifies that in the early days of his ministry he and Sarah learnt to trust God in all situations because when they started to go out to preach the gospel and plant churches they had no money or means of support. They literally had nothing, but had made a choice to do what they knew was God's will for them. They sought to obey the Great Commission given by the Lord Jesus to His disciples in Matthew 28: 18-20 (NIV).

"Then Jesus came to them and said, 'All authority in heaven and on earth has been given to me. Therefore go and make disciples of all nations, baptizing them in the name of the Father and of the Son and of the Holy Spirit, and teaching them to obey everything I have commanded you. And surely I am with you always, to the very end of the age.'"

So Emmy and Sarah did just that. They left their home tribal area, went to an area of Uganda where many people had not heard the gospel and began to preach and teach. People were saved and churches planted, but in the course of this ministry they came across many children who were suffering. This led them into another kind of ministry – taking care of the poor and needy children around them. Emmy and Sarah had no financial resources to do this, just hearts that overflowed with love and a willingness to try to alleviate the pain of the children. The Lord took the offering of their love and has grown the ministry to what it is today. Looking back over the past years they acknowledge that it was not by their own wisdom or strength, but by the power and grace of God that the ministry has grown to care for so many children. Sarah and Emmy just kneel before the Lord in praise and adoration for all He has done. As they look to the future, they know that the Scripture in Philippians 1:6 is a promise for them: "Being confident of this, that he who began a good work in you will carry it on to completion until the day of Christ Jesus" (NIV).

I had asked Emmy if he struggled at all with cultural differences when he was working with Europeans and Americans. His answer was so typical of his godly attitude: "Be honest – that way we can be better partners together. I am also aware of how faithful God has been ever since He called me into this ministry.

1 Thessalonians 5:24: "The one who calls you is faithful and he will do it" (NIV).

Emmy said, "The Lord connected me with the right people in the UK and USA, giving them the same burden and together things have been accomplished. To be honest, I have made a lot of mistakes, but His grace has been with me, prompting me to realize this and correct them.

"There are so many reasons why I cannot doubt that it is God who connected us with all the sponsors with whom we work in PCM, because the cultural differences could frustrate them as they work alongside us, but God has given them the grace to be patient as we learn to appreciate each other's culture and way of doing things. This has helped me to know how to do things in the right way."

"When the work first began it was not organised and did not have a name. It was just a matter of taking care of children in our home – an extended family. However, when we had more than forty children in the house, our neighbours around us began to ask questions and we realized that we needed to be registered with the government and do things in an official way. It was then that we thought about registering as a charity the name, 'Parental Care Ministry', because our main aim was to give parental love to these children."

"I do thank God," Emmy continues, "I thank Him for my wife, Sarah, who has been such a great help, sharing the vision and working with me. I also thank our biological children, Grace, Faith, Daniel, Roger and Julie, for being so good and loving all their brothers and sisters in the extended family without ever making them feel different or unwanted. They, too, truly have a heart of love for other children.

As a family, we have shared together and faced the problems and challenges as they arose, learning together to trust God to take us through them. It is very humbling to look back and see just how far the Lord has brought us, and we give all the glory back to Him."

I had also asked Pastor Emmy to share his vision for the future of PCM. He feels the work has reached a stage where there is a great need to be concerned for the future. It has grown so much and so quickly. His concern is that it will continue to grow, but above all, remain spiritually healthy. If the focus of the schools does not remain totally God-centred and they become just a humanitarian project, then they will fail. Emmy and Sarah feel that it is now time to pass the vision on to the next generation. Some of the children who first came to them are now young adults and they are in line to be future leaders of PCM. These young people are being mentored and grounded in the Word of God in order that they will build strong foundations for their lives and future ministries. Emmy and Sarah pray that in the future they will be able to pass the baton on to them to continue the work in God's way. For now they are teaching them these five principles for their lives:

1. To put Jesus as number one in their lives, according to the teaching of Matthew 6:33, (NIV): "But seek first his kingdom and his righteousness, and all these things will be given to you as well."

2. To study, live and proclaim God's Word. Ezra 7:10: "For Ezra had devoted himself to the study and observance of the Law of the Lord, and to teaching its decrees and laws" (NIV).

3. To study well academically and gain qualifications to be doctors, engineers, teachers etc., not necessarily to return to PCM, but trusting that some will return to work there.

4. To always take PCM as their real family and as such stay connected.

5. To demonstrate the Father's love in action by helping others in need.

The sign of a truly great man is his willingness to share his gifts and vision with others and to be ready, when the time comes, to step back and let someone else take the baton and run with it. Already, Emmy is working towards this. Along with him and Sarah we would join in the old hymn of praise:

> How good is the God we adore,
> Our faithful, unchangeable friend,
> His love is as great as His power
> And knows neither measure nor end.
>
> For Christ is the first and the last,
> His Spirit will guide us safe home
> We'll praise Him for all that is past
> And trust Him for all that's to come

If you have read this book and wish to learn more or sponsor a child in a PCM school, please look at the website:

www.pcmuk.org

Lightning Source UK Ltd.
Milton Keynes UK
UKOW06f1118130416

272162UK00001B/43/P